—A—
MILLION
WARS

To: Dan

Charles E. "Chuck" Ferguson
16 Dec 2017

CHARLES E. "CHUCK" FERGUSON

PAGE PUBLISHING, INC.
New York, NY

First originally published by Page Publishing, Inc. 2017

ISBN 978-1-64027-574-4 (Paperback)
ISBN 978-1-64027-575-1 (Digital)

Printed in the United States of America

FOREWORD

Charles E. "Chuck" Ferguson believes there's a different meaning and understanding of war for each combat veteran who's asked what it's like.

Ferguson's answer is "cold, hot, lonely, sick, tired and scared."

An Armored Cavalry officer in Vietnam, Ferguson takes readers on his twelve-month journey from his arrival at a staging area for combat operations into Cambodia to the day he safely returned home to his family in Harrah, Ok.

He began his tour of duty as a second lieutenant assigned as a commander of an Armored Cavalry platoon of the Eleventh Cavalry "Blackhorse Regiment" and was soon promoted to the rank of first lieutenant.

Ferguson is a modest man; his reason for writing the book is to publicly acknowledge "all who serve and have served in our armed forces."

The retired Army Reserve Lieutenant Colonel hopes younger Americans will understand better the sacrifices made by others for our country. He also hopes to understand himself better to connect with fellow veterans by affording them a way they can reflect on their own lives and experiences.

His descriptions of events are vivid despite being a first-time author.

A reader almost can see the firecracker-like "beautiful fountain" that Ferguson first viewed in the combat area and quickly learned was a deadly incoming phosphorous mortar round, signaling a heavy enemy mortar attack.

Later he takes readers with him on a platoon reconnaissance mission. Along a creek bed, they found what very likely was an enemy tunnel. Ferguson cleared the tunnel with grenades.

The Oklahoma State University and Reserve Officer Training Corps (ROTC) graduate urges readers to realize his book is "one man's memories" intended to be historically and technically accurate without embellishment.

Ferguson purposely omits discussion of specific wounds. Always a soldier, he does not reveal the full names of those soldiers in his platoon, choosing to protect their privacy.

In his book readers will learn how close fighting men are each other and how they watch each other's back in combat.

Like so many combat veterans, Ferguson doesn't discuss combat awards or how they were earned except in a passage about finding a stack of papers on a high shelf in an empty former headquarters building.

Those papers shocked him. They were documents awarding him a second Bronze Star.

He wrote nothing else about the award or any others he'd received.

John Greiner
Col. USAR (retired)

PREFACE

As promised in the Bible, throughout history there have always been wars and rumors of war.

War comes in all sizes and levels of intensity. They are fought in all climates and under all conditions known to man. The common denominator is the word *man*, and increasingly today, *woman*.

Although technology has been advanced and utilized in most, if not all conflicts, it is always the soldier who is charged with getting the job done. The politicians and indigenous peoples are affected and often have a great impact on the outcome of the conflict. It still remains the job of the soldier to take whatever actions are necessary to eventually achieve the goals, real or perceived, necessary to end the hostilities in the most favorable manner for their side of the conflict.

As a combat veteran, I am often asked questions about my wartime experiences. What they really want to know is "What is war like?" The answer I give is that I only know about one war. The truth is that of all the millions who have served, there is a different meaning and understanding of war for each one.

When asked "What is it like to be a soldier in combat?" my answer is "cold, hot, lonely, sick, tired, and scared." Notwithstanding the conditions in which the soldier serves, the human spirit is resilient, and the soldier can actually learn to enjoy his friends and, for the most part, find some measure of happiness.

There are many reasons soldiers make the sacrifices they do. Among them, of course, are patriotism, love of family, loyalty to their comrades in arms, and many more reasons known only to the individual soldier.

Everything we do is done for a reason. That said I have asked myself, why would I expend the time and effort required to write this preface and all the pages that follow? The answers are clear to me:

> This is intended to be a positive acknowledgment of all who serve and have served in our armed forces.

> It is a method of providing a recorded legacy, as a part of my history, to allow members of my family and friends to have some understanding of who I am and why I have lived my life as I have.

> Hopefully, younger Americans will be inspired by a better understanding of the sacrifices made by others to do what they can to protect this wonderful country in which we live and the freedoms so rare and dear to us.

> It is my intent to connect with my fellow veterans and, in some way, give them an opportunity to reflect on their own lives and experiences and to be entertained in the process.

> Perhaps the most important aspect for me, personally, is the process of reflection and analysis to help me better understand myself.

As you read the following pages, please bear in mind that these are one man's memories. I have made an attempt to be historically and technically accurate and have guarded against embellishment of any situation. To the contrary, I have purposely omitted references to specific wounds and other generally unpleasant circumstances of war. The names of a number of my fellow soldiers have been omitted to protect their right to privacy. If they want others to know who they are and what they did, it is their war and their decision.

As already indicated, each soldier experiences his own war. These pages are an attempt to tell a part of the story through one man's eyes.

THE JOURNEY BEGINS

The day had finally arrived. After Armor Officer Basic Training at Fort Knox and almost a year of practicing to become an effective armored cavalry platoon leader, it was time to say goodbye to my family and friends. My orders directed me to fly from Oklahoma City to Travis Air Force Base in California.

The goodbyes, I now know, were especially difficult for my father, who had served his combat time in Europe during World War II. He did not know the specifics, but he understood the perils and hardships before me. He earned his retirement as a US Army Colonel.

As a young Second Lieutenant, I, of course, did not really know what to expect. My confidence was at a high level, and the opportunity to prove myself loomed large.

The commercial flight to San Francisco was uneventful with one notable exception. The seat next to me was occupied by a US Army Captain. He was a helicopter pilot en route to S. Vietnam for his second tour of duty. He was not very talkative and was obviously not happy to be returning for further combat. He frankly said he did not expect to survive the tour of duty. I have often thought of him and hope he did return for a full and happy life. That said, it was not an encouraging experience for me; however, the exuberance of youth prevailed, and I moved forward with anticipation.

After a layover at Travis Air Force Base, where my aunt and uncle entertained me with a whirlwind visit to San Francisco, and brief stops in Hawaii and Guam, we arrived in S. Vietnam. As I stepped from the plane, I was shocked to see a large and very busy airport. Nothing about it told me I was in a war zone other than the large number of uniformed personnel. The stench was strong and the heat and humidity were oppressive. I knew I was not in Oklahoma anymore. We boarded a bus and soon arrived at the processing station to receive our unit assignments.

I was assigned to the Eleventh Cavalry "Blackhorse Regiment" and within about twenty-four hours was transported to Dian Base Camp for a week of "newbie" training.

Dian was a large post with lots of semipermanent structures. There were numerous bunkers and lots of sandbags. It was a little boring, and as I would come to understand, the training checked the required administrative blocks but was not necessarily what I would need. The chow was great, and we had good dry cots to sleep on.

When the time came for the next leg of the journey, several Lieutenants and I put our duffel bags on top of a deuce and a half truck loaded with supplies. That is also where we rode. We were quite nervous as it was a long convoy through the countryside to Lai Khe, where we spent the night. We still had not been issued personal weapons and felt very vulnerable.

The next day we rode the same vehicle to *Quan Loi*. That is where we got our first true sense that we were in a war zone. *Quan Loi* was a forward staging area for operations in Cambodia. The traffic on the dirt airstrip was amazing as we watched a nonstop parade of cargo aircraft landing, being unloaded without stopping and taking off again presumably to get a new load of supplies. A few mortar rounds landed on the edge of the airport and definitely got our attention. I knew I had a lot to learn when I noticed that the personnel working the air base paid little or no attention to the incoming rounds. They were apparently used to incoming fire.

We were finally issued personal .45-caliber pistols and after about two hours' delay were told to get on a resupply Huey helicopter for the trip to our unit. We were soon deposited at the Third Squadron Field Headquarters somewhere in Cambodia.

The squadron headquarters was a combat headquarters consisting of a number of command vehicles and protected by armored personnel carriers, tanks, and artillery. We were interviewed as a group by the Squadron Commander and were given our individual assignments. I was puzzled that the squadron commander pushed me to accept the position of HHT executive officer instead of being a combat platoon leader. He agreed to honor my strong desire to function as a combat platoon leader. I will never know whether he thought I would make a strong executive officer or was concerned that I would not be a good choice for an armored cavalry platoon leader. Fortunately, he later let me know that it was a good choice to give me a platoon leadership position.

We were dispersed for the night to individual armored vehicles (tracks) on the perimeter. It was an exciting night. Intelligence indicated the probability of a major attack that night. We were up all night delivering interdictory fires to prevent massing of enemy troops. I was given an M79 grenade launcher and fired a very large number of grenades. Based on the large cut and significant amount of blood on my hand, I figured out that I was not holding the weapon properly. This, of course, was only one of many practical lessons yet to be experienced. No attack came.

My friend Bob and I were both assigned to L Troop, Third Squadron, Eleventh Cavalry. We boarded a Huey helicopter early that morning and were flown to L Troop Headquarters in the jungle somewhere near *Snuol,* Cambodia.

The Headquarters vehicles and one platoon were circled in a clearing with tall bamboo on one side and a trail on the other. As we prepared to land, Cpt. Ralph Miles, the troop commander, walked out to meet us. We were careful not to salute. Bob and I both knew that in a similar circumstance, one of our fellow platoon leaders at Fort Hood had saluted when he got off the helicopter. He was immediately killed by a sniper. We learned later that he too had been reporting to Captain Miles.

Captain Miles led us to the command track, where he briefed us and assigned us to our platoons. I was joined by the then platoon leader of Third Platoon, of which I was to assume leadership.

I thought it had been a long and exciting journey thus far. Little did I know the journey was only beginning.

BAPTISM OF FIRE

Fortunately, I was able to ride along with the current Third Platoon leader for two days and nights before he was promoted and moved to a different troop. He was a likeable fellow and seemed to do his best to ensure my orientation was effective. He was killed in action a short time after going to his new assignment.

The first night seemed uneventful except for the strange noises, including the crackling of growing bamboo, which can sound a lot like a gunshot in the darkness. We ensured that at least one person on each vehicle was awake and on guard duty. There were four crewmen on each vehicle, which meant we each had roughly two hours of guard duty if things remained quiet.

Sometime around 0200 hours we heard a loud explosion. I was told it was an "automatic ambush" that had been triggered. An "automatic ambush" consisted of claymore mines, a battery, and a trip wire mechanism. When properly deployed on a trail or avenue of approach, it was extremely effective in killing the enemy or at least providing early warning.

When daylight came, Third Platoon was deployed to investigate the site of the explosion. It was clear that enemy soldiers had been injured in the blast. There was only one body remaining at the site. A few of our experienced troopers used ropes and grappling hooks to roll the body over and check for booby traps. We soon discovered a hastily dug burial site that contained a number of enemy bodies. It was our unpleasant task to exhume the remains and search them for intelligence materials. For someone who had never seen a body outside of a funeral home this was a sobering task. I began the natural internal process of differentiating between friendly and enemy casualties. Such processes are necessary psychological events to steel one against the difficulties of war.

Later that day, L Troop was ordered to a new position. On the way we passed the ruins of *Snuol. Snuol* had been the site of a major battle a few days earlier. It was hard for me to believe this had once been a thriving village.

When we arrived at our new position, we were pleasantly surprised to find the engineers had used bulldozers to push up a berm about six feet high and forming a large circle. The berm was high enough to provide some protection for our vehicles but not high enough to interfere with our weapons or field of vision. We deployed along the inside of the berm and were to provide protection for a large number of engineers and L Troop Headquarters. The jungle had been pushed back from the berm leaving about one hundred feet of open space for fields of fire. Beyond that were huge piles of bulldozed trees and then the jungle. We would soon learn the piles of trees offered great protection to enemy soldiers.

As night fell, we ate our rations and prepared for the night. Much to my surprise, two cots appeared for the use of the current platoon leader and myself. The back ramp of the APC was dropped allowing us to sleep with our upper bodies inside the vehicle and the remainder extended on the ramp. I did not particularly like the arrangement as I felt a platoon leader should live in the same circumstances as his troops.

Sometime during the night all were awakened by very loud noises. As I opened my eyes I saw a beautiful fountain a few yards behind our track. It looked like a fourth of July display. It soon became apparent that the fountain was one of many incoming phosphorous mortar rounds. We were under heavy attack by mortars and direct weapons fire.

The driver immediately started the engine and raised the ramp to protect against shrapnel. That was the end of the cots, which were smashed in the ramp. That was fine with me. The protection was much more important than a silly cot. From then on I slept on the ammunition boxes in the bottom of the vehicle just like everyone else except the driver who always remained in the driver's seat.

The fire-fight was intense and lasted for some time. Welcome to the shooting war.

THIRD PLATOON

The other Lieutenant departed for his new assignment and I was the proud but nervous leader of a combat armored cavalry platoon.

The platoon was comprised of seven ACAVs and three Sheridan Tanks. The ACAVs were standard armored personnel carriers that had been armed with two M60 machine guns manned by the two crewman who stood behind the cupola through an open hatch and a .50-caliber machine gun operated by the track commander in the cupola. The driver usually fired a hand held M79 grenade launcher. All personnel were also armed with M16 rifles except the platoon leader who was issued a .45-caliber pistol. The M60 machine guns had armored shields in front of them and were fired through a hole in the shield. Each ACAV vehicle had a 4 man crew and the Sheridans had three-man crew resulting in a platoon contingent of approximately thirty-seven troopers. The school solution indicated the armored cavalry platoon had firepower equivalent to an infantry battalion. It was a formidable fighting force.

The platoon leader's track, on which I rode, had the standard crew and armament with the exception of an extra radio and antennae. It always bothered me that it was the only platoon vehicle with two antennae. That was like painting a big red bullseye on the side saying this is a commander's vehicle. Needless to say, the enemy liked to target vehicles with two antennae.

There were, of course, a variety of personalities in the platoon. I learned to love and care for them all to the best of my ability. Some of us would not have been friends in the civilian world, but in combat things change greatly. Each trooper knows he must support and be supported by everyone else. We also found many commonalities that would not exist anywhere other than a combat arena. It hurts that I cannot remember many of their names, but I can remember their faces and who they really were. I will always be indebted to each and every one of them.

The track commander duties on my track were handled by a great young man we called Woody. This allowed me to plan, analyze, direct fires, talk on multiple radio nets, fire my M60 machine gun, read the map, and it seemed like a million other things in the heat of combat.

Woody was a mainstay for me, especially in the initial days, when there was so much for me to learn and no time to learn it. He was not afraid to suggest courses of action or to let me know what he thought we were facing. He had been through a large number of firefights.

There were a number of other leaders in the platoon who were invaluable. Some of these will be addressed later.

THE CAMBODIAN VILLAGERS

Our area of operations in Cambodia is a beautiful tropical country with an unending supply of green vibrant jungle, small villages, and some rice paddies. The climate is wet and warm.

The Cambodian people we met were natives reminiscent of those featured in National Geographic Magazine when I was a boy. They had few possessions and only wanted a chance to live their lives without interference from the Viet Cong or from us.

The typical village consisted of a few bamboo and grass huts built on stilts. The few pigs and ducks they had were housed either in separate grass sheds, or more often, in the space under the family living space. There were no stores in which to shop, hospitals, or schools. The few roads in the area were dirt and not maintained. It appeared to be pretty much a matter of self sustainment in all things for the villagers.

It was enlightening to note that one particular village was considered fortunate to be able to provide the village chief with a bicycle. The bicycle was the only means of travel to other villages other than walking. Because of the general lack of roads, the bicycle was ridden on ages old jungle trails. We worry about being delayed in a traffic jam?

The Cambodian villagers were a simple but very pleasant people. They had little but sought ways to share what they could. When we first arrived, it was apparent that not all the men and even young boys were present. This was a matter of concern to us because of their potential to be enemy soldiers. As we patrolled the area around the first village, we encountered a group of Cambodian men and boys. We kept our weapons at the ready while our interpreter questioned them. We soon learned that they had fled the village in fear of us. The Viet Cong had convinced them that we would kill them when we came. Thankfully, we were able to convince them that we would do them no harm and they returned to their village.

There were a number of interactions with the villagers resulting in surprises to us because we had never truly imagined that people on this planet lived the way they did.

The village chief was very effective in expressing his gratitude for treating his people well. One afternoon, as we were passing close to the village, the chief and a few others stood by the trail. He had something in his outstretched hands that was obviously meant to be a gift for us. Much to our surprise, it was a very old and severely damaged M79 grenade launcher that was of absolutely no value. To the chief, however, it was something he treasured and he felt we would treasure the gift. We did treasure the gift because of the good intent of the chief and his people.

On one occasion, we were required to search the village for weapons or other supplies hidden there by the Viet Cong. We did not like having to do the search because we had so quickly learned to appreciate the villagers. Our medic was doing his best to tend to any minor medical needs the villagers might have, when he came upon a young mother caring for her very sick baby. The medic diagnosed the problem and tried to give the baby needed medicine. The mother became very fearful and would not let the medic administer the medicine. Our interpreter soon discovered that the Viet Cong had convinced her that we would poison the children. The quick thinking medic handled the situation perfectly. He placed two pills in his hand and through the interpreter asked the mother to take one of the pills from his hand. He immediately swallowed the remaining pill to prove to her that it was not poison. She then helped the baby swallow the medicine.

Seeing the sick baby reminded me of one my earliest personal memories. So many things made me think of home at the strangest times. When I was a small toddler, I'm sure not speaking yet, my family lived in a small house in Oklahoma City. I somehow managed to sneak out through the front door and make my way to the middle of the street just as a city bus was approaching. It was no problem for me. I sat down in the middle of the street and raised my hand to demand he stop. Fortunately, the driver did stop and vigorously honked the bus horn. Needless to say my father arrived hastily and removed me from the street without harm other than the stern scolding I received. To this day I wonder if my decision to stop the bus was an early sign of a leadership trait to control the situation or if I was simply to dumb to know better.

We seemed to get daily lessons telling us that although people are in different circumstance from those to which we are accustomed to, most people want to live their lives doing the right thing. We just have to "seek to understand."

CAMBODIA NDP

The area west of *Snuol* was undoubtedly beautiful in more peaceful times. We found the area to be dirty and battle scarred in many places. It was the rainy season, and the mud was terrible because of all the armored vehicle traffic.

The troop NDP was established along a main road. The clearing for the NDP was made using bulldozers to push up a large berm and to push the huge brush piles about a hundred feet beyond the berm. The NDP was much larger than normal because of our mission of protecting a large number of combat engineers.

Cambodia had been used by the enemy as a safe haven for some time and was their primary base for resupply of their efforts in S. Vietnam. The enemy was large in number and determined to deny us access to the area.

The first few days were spent performing various search-and-destroy missions from which we normally returned to the NDP at dusk. The jungles were heavy and made our missions difficult.

I distinctly remember passing the Squadron NDP on one afternoon. A chinook helicopter had crashed and burned at the site either because of mechanical failure or enemy fire. I was told the casualties were heavy.

We were always on high alert in the NDP. It seemed to be a nightly occurrence to receive incoming mortar and rocket fire. We would always respond with a heavy volume of fire to counter any enemy troops that might be trying to break through our defenses.

Shortly after establishment of the NDP we received a very heavy rocket and mortar attack. The incoming fire was accurate and devastating. I was called immediately to the command track for a briefing. As I left the command track, I was taken aback to see approximately forty wounded soldiers receiving first aid. Most of them were engineers. The large number of engineers for whom we were providing security constituted a lucrative target for the enemy gunners. I paused only briefly before returning to my platoon. It was obvious that we were in for a serious fight. Fortunately, we repelled a large number of enemy soldiers and the fight lasted only about one hour.

A few days later we were the recipients of yet another very heavy rocket and mortar barrage. It was early afternoon and the day was hot. As we returned fire, little did we know this would be probably the biggest and toughest battle we would see.

It was clear that a large number of enemy troops were attacking our NDP and the Squadron NDP simultaneously. The troop commander was on a search-and-destroy mission, and I was in charge of the NDP defense until his return. I remember thinking that I then knew how the soldiers at the Alamo felt. That was a fleeting thought but very sobering. I knew we were in a tough fight.

Incoming small arms and Rocket Propelled Grenade fire were very heavy as was incoming mortar fire. Because of the vegetation and old brush piles, we seldom saw the enemy but certainly sensed their presence from their accurate fires. At one point I saw the "green basketball," an incoming RPG strike the berm a few feet to my left. The loud crack of the explosion rendered me deaf in my left ear for about three days. There was nothing I could do about it except maintain the fight.

Our troopers were well trained and took the necessary actions with only minimal direction from me. In order to be prepared for a possible breach of our lines, I designated sections around the perimeter to be ready to move instantly upon order to reinforce the weakened sector of the perimeter. The plan was to move every other track in that sector to ensure no sector was totally abandoned. Fortunately, I did not have to implement that plan.

As the hours passed and the heavy fighting continued, we began to run low on .50-caliber machine-gun ammunition. To conserve ammunition, I would periodically issue orders to cease firing the .50-caliber machine guns. The action conserved ammunition, but had the expected result. Incoming fire would increase dramatically in volume and accuracy. It was obvious the enemy feared the .50-caliber machine guns.

Night was approaching and the ferocity of the battle increased. It was readily apparent that the enemy was massing troops for a major push on our position. I was happy to learn that the troop commander had returned to our position and was in charge of the defensive efforts.

We received an order I experienced only that one time and never want to experience again. We were ordered to "button up." That meant we were to close all hatches on our tracks leaving only a small crack to relieve pressure if the track took a direct hit. The troop commander had requested "danger close artillery airburst" to eliminate enemy soldiers close to our position. Unfortunately, the likelihood of our being hit by shrapnel from our own artillery was very great.

Because the Squadron NDP, about one kilometer away, was under heavy attack, we knew we were on our own except for supporting artillery and helicopter gunships.

About dusk, I witnessed one of the most effective and difficult coordinated attacks I could ever imagine. We were running low on ammunition and had amassed a number of wounded to be evacuated. In order to bring in resupply helicopters and evacuate the wounded, the volume of enemy fire had to be suppressed. Upon the troop commander's orders we ceased firing from all our tracks. We witnessed the spectacle of a massive artillery barrage just outside of our perimeter at the same time as several cobra attack helicopters delivered numerous rockets and machine gun fire into the enemy positions. In order to avoid being hit by the incoming artillery rounds, the attack helicopters approached just above and at an angle parallel to the arced path of the artillery rounds being fired from our squadron NDP 155 Howitzer battery. The action was incredibly dangerous but effective.

The resupply helicopters were able to approach from the side of the perimeter away from the barrage. Their approach was obviously very dangerous, but they managed to provide the much needed ammunition resupply and evacuate the wounded. The bravery of the pilots involved was incredible to me but not surprising. Soldiers find a way to do what has to be done to save their fellow soldiers.

Having been resupplied, we were able to continue the fight. A few hours later the enemy withdrew. Our intelligence section at higher headquarters later estimated that we had been under siege from an entire NVA division. I just knew we had faced a large number of well trained and disciplined enemy troops. It had been a difficult and costly fight, but thanks to technology and the cunning and bravery of the US soldiers and airmen, the fight was won.

THE TOOL BAG

Everyone knows that soldiers are well disciplined and tidy people. All soldiers learn to keep their personal and group areas clean and in good order. Their socks are rolled and placed as neatly as possible in the soldier's trunk or dresser. Skill at making the bedding on a cot tight enough to bounce a quarter on it is a goal of most, if not all, soldiers. Soldiers care for their equipment and weapons for these items are required to enable them to do their job, and in many cases, sustain life itself.

There are, of course, exceptions to the general rule of tidiness. The exceptions are understandable, but not necessarily acceptable. The maintenance of equipment and personal items can have a profound effect on the soldier's war fighting capability. As the platoon leader it was part of my job to ensure that all areas and equipment were reasonably neat and in the best working condition possible in the circumstances. This duty was not always fulfilled.

In our NDP (night defensive position) somewhere near *Snuol* Cambodia, we were cold, wet, and muddy. It was mid-afternoon and I noticed a small canvas tool bag containing a few wrenches had been left on the top of the APC just behind the cupola. Wet tools and the strong possibility that they would be lost if we had to move quickly, were not acceptable. I did not know who had left the tools there. It really did not matter. Woody, the track commander, was ultimately responsible for the equipment and the actions of the crew maintaining the equipment. Woody was a fantastic track commander, but the problem had to be brought to his attention.

Before I could say anything to Woody, incoming mortar and small arms fire began to pour into our position. The battle was long and difficult. We coordinated our machine gun and tank fire with the artillery and helicopter support groups.

In combat, a soldier understands that he is in harm's way. The effective soldier pushes that worry to the back of his mind and concentrates on doing his particular job.

At one point during the battle, three AK-47 rounds struck the top of the APC somewhere in front of me. I was momentarily blinded by debris generated by the incoming rounds, but was able to quickly recover and continue my tasks of firing my machine gun and directing the platoon.

Eventually the incoming fire stopped, and the battle was over at least for a time. As we began to reload and take stock of our situation, I noticed the canvas tool bag was in a little different position. Closer examination showed it now had three bullet holes in it. Considering the alignment of the bullet holes, it became clear that I had been the intended target. Had the tool bag been stored properly, I would have been the recipient of three AK-47 rounds in my torso. Somehow, the debris in my eyes and the fact that someone did not properly store the tool bag, did not seem like such a big deal. Some would say I was lucky. Some say it was divine guidance looking out for me. I don't believe in luck, so you figure it out. This was not my only inexplicable escape from harm.

THE GULCH

It was a typical day. We were on a multi platoon patrol searching a rubber plantation. Our goal was to find and engage the enemy or at least locate his supply stashes. Our mission is best described in the painted words on every Eleventh Cavalry combat vehicle. The words were there as a result of an order by a previous regimental commander, Col Patton. Col Patton, who later was promoted to be a general officer, was the son of the famous World War II general George Patton. The words were: "Standing order of the day. Find the bastards and kill them." Crude but accurate and to the point. We were expected to eliminate the enemy threat, and that, of course, necessitated finding the very elusive enemy.

Third Platoon soon came upon a rather fast flowing shallow stream in a gulch approximately twenty feet deep with sloping grassy sides. That was the only clean and fast flowing stream I recall seeing in my entire tour of duty.

Standing in the middle of the stream was an Asian man who I guessed to be in his late twenties. The man was much larger than the local Cambodians and appeared to be in good physical condition. He was scantily clothed as he appeared to have removed most of them and was washing them in the stream. Apparently we had surprised him. If he was an enemy soldier, there was no place for him to hide in a rubber plantation. The rubber plantation was made up of rows and rows of trees with high tops and only minimal vegetation beneath the shade of forest canopy. It did not seem correct that he was in that location miles from the nearest village and without weapons or tools.

Our interpreter questioned him without a satisfactory explanation as to who he was and why he was there. We took him into custody and had him escorted to our headquarters. I will never know for sure, but I now believe that he was a Chinese soldier supporting the Viet Cong. I understand that the Chinese Army was not involved in the conflict. I don't understand how we identified more than one dead enemy soldier as Chinese if they weren't there.

The day was not done and I was destined to learn more lessons the hard way.

Third Platoon was ordered to form a dismounted patrol to move downstream in the creek bed on a reconnaissance mission. The patrol included me and about ten troopers. The remaining men of the platoon stayed with the vehicles. It was not a pleasant task, but, was obviously necessary. The creek bed was deep enough and the banks steep enough that we could not see or contact our platoon vehicles except by radio. That meant that the firepower of the platoon vehicles was not accessible to us in the event of trouble.

After we had gone down the creek bed a few hundred yards, a small finger of the creek bed went off to the left about fifty feet. The finger, or draw as I prefer to call it, was about thirty to forty feet across and had a significant amount of grass. The grass was not tall, but was sufficient to conceal anyone or anything that might be there. I soon realized that I had moved my men into a potential killing zone. I dispersed my men as best I could. As we searched the area we soon discovered the opening to a tunnel. If the tunnel was occupied, there could easily have been other tunnels and fighting positions in the draw. We were essentially in the lower side of a natural bowl and would have been easy pickings for any enemy soldiers.

Having discovered the tunnel, it was evident that it was a source of immediate danger and had to be quickly neutralized. Since I was the closest to the tunnel, about six feet away, I pulled the pin on a hand grenade, crawled to the tunnel and threw in the grenade. That was the first grenade I had thrown in a combat situation. Please remember that war is not very clear. I did not know if the tunnel was occupied, empty, or even an ammunition area filled with explosives. I hurriedly crawled back from the tunnel entrance and waited for the grenade to explode. Nothing happened. I tried to gather my wits and determined the only thing to do was to deploy another grenade. This time I was better prepared. I remembered to remove both safety latching mechanism and the safety pin on the grenade before throwing it. The crawl back to the tunnel was not enjoyable. Would the first grenade be thrown back at me? Would I come face-to-face with an AK-47 rifle? The imagination is hard to control when one is stressed out. The second grenade was deposited in the tunnel and exploded just like it was supposed to do. Isn't it amazing how much better things work when we follow instructions?

Fortunately, we were ordered not to go in the tunnel and proceeded to clear the rest of the draw. We then radioed our platoon vehicles that we were coming out of the creek bed. It was good to see them close by, but, we all knew we had been lucky. They could have done little to help us had we been ambushed.

From that day forward I was always vigilant when approaching an unfamiliar area. I would always plan as if I were the enemy and then prepare a plan for us to counter that threat. Can't say I was perfect at it, but, the planning greatly helped us in many difficult encounters.

FIREFLIES

The majority of people seem inclined to believe that a soldier is always busy. The truth is that the majority of time spent in combat is basically idle. Even though many events occur that require hours on end of hard work and one must always be prepared for what will inevitably happen without notice, many hours are spent waiting in a generally uncomfortable environment. Whether hot or cold, rainy or dry, someone must always be on guard.

Guard duty at night is especially difficult. On our tracks, at least one person was always alert in the cupola and manning the .50-caliber machine gun. Soldiers in the field are generally sleep deprived, tired from endless hours of physically and mentally demanding work, and often sick. It seems almost impossible to sit quietly and remain awake and vigilant. One trick I soon learned was to rest my elbow and my hand in such a way that if I nodded off, my chin would strike the sharp metal above the butterfly trigger on the .50-caliber machine gun. It sounds crude, but it always kept me awake and reasonably alert. Sleeping guards are not acceptable in a combat zone.

There are some good things to be said about the ability to observe nature in total quietness and darkness. The fireflies were abundant and made a beautiful and interesting show in the darkness. Having been raised in the Oklahoma country-side, I often felt fortunate to enjoy the stars without interference from city lights. However, in the Cambodian jungle, the pleasure of truly seeing the stars was revealed to me. There were, of course, no lights anywhere near to dim the view of the stars. It was an incredible experience to view the stars and enjoy the peace of total quiet. These times were very special to me.

The technology was not very well developed, but we were provided with night vision devices we knew as "starlight" scopes. Many hours of staring into darkness results in an over active imagination causing the viewer to see movement and objects that just are not really there. The scopes magnified the light and provided a blurry green view. They were not perfect but were a definite improvement over the naked eye alone.

The North Vietnamese Army and the Viet Cong used a green lens in their flashlights unlike US Army forces who used a red lens. The colored lens decreased the light emitted but provided the distinct advantage of being more difficult for others to see the source of the light.

The enemy's use of the green lens was a definite problem for us. If we saw a series of small green specks of light, it was our inclination to believe it was the enemy either working in a specific area or using the lights to move along a trail and watch for booby traps. The problem became evident when one peered into the darkness through a starlight scope. Each of the numerous fireflies looked as though it could be an enemy flashlight. There was no good way to discern the difference between a firefly and a flashlight. We will never know how many fireflies were killed using .50-caliber machine guns. Better to be careful than dead.

HOT GUNS

On our ACAVs the most effective weapon was undoubtedly the .50-caliber machine gun operated by the track commander. It gave us the firepower and rate of fire to make a difference. The difference was not difficult to perceive. When we were able to place effective fire on the enemy, the enemy's rate of fire and accuracy was greatly decreased.

Our tracks were always loaded with two to three layers of ammunition cans on the floor. This normally was enough to allow maximum firing of all weapons. In a few instances, when the firefight lasted for hours, our supply of .50-caliber ammunition ran low. As a result I had to order limited use of the .50-caliber machine guns to ensure we had enough ammunition to repel a major attack by the enemy. As soon as we decreased the rate of fire from the .50 calibers, the volume of enemy fire would increase significantly. It did not take a genius to figure out the .50 calibers were a very effective weapon.

On several occasions, during major and protracted firefights, the barrels of the .50 calibers would become overheated. The result was that instead of shooting where aimed, we could see by the tracers that the rounds were going out in an ever widening coil pattern. Obviously our effectiveness was degraded.

The troopers had two solutions for the overheated barrels. Neither solution was a textbook solution, but was the result of good old American ingenuity.

The first solution consisted of keeping several canteens of used engine oil near the gun. As the barrel got hot, the gunner would simply pour oil on the barrel to cool the metal. Pouring the oil required caution because the oil would ignite into flames two to three feet high. Contact with those flames would instantly burn the trooper. It was a simple solution that worked well to prolong the barrel life of the gun.

Eventually, if fired long enough, the barrel would fail even with the use of oil for coolant. The second solution was to replace the barrel with the spare barrel all troopers kept in their tracks. It only took a few seconds to throw the old barrel off to the ground, using heavy gloves, and replace it with the new barrel. Now the second barrel was not actually authorized to be kept in readiness. That did not stop the troopers from ensuring they always had a spare. Somehow, in combat, troopers tended to worry more about staying alive than they worried about complying with army supply regulations.

MEMORIAL SERVICE

The only field memorial service I was able to attend was held at our squadron fire base near *Snuol*, Cambodia. My platoon happened to be securing the base camp that day, which meant I was available.

The day was hot, it had not rained all day, and the scene was very rugged. We had endured several attacks at the firebase resulting in numerous shell craters, no vegetation, and lots of used ammo boxes and other litter. Everything was covered in deep red mud, and of course, the business of war went on. Crew were either on guard duty, re-supplying, performing maintenance, or tending to some of the other myriad duties that never seemed to end.

I will always be thankful that, despite many engagements, to my knowledge no trooper assigned to me was killed in action. That does not mean that others around me did not lose their lives doing their duty.

On this day, we were honoring the memories of three fallen soldiers who had been killed at our base camp. I cannot recall for sure, but I believe two were troopers and one was an engineer. It does not matter what their duties or what we called them, they were our brothers in arms.

The service was held outside on the muddy ground. Three M16 rifles with bayonets had been pushed into the ground in a row. A soldier's helmet rested atop the butt of each rifle.

The attendees were comprised of a few officers and NCOs, a few of the honored soldiers' friends, and a few other soldiers who wanted to show their respect for their fallen comrades. In total, I believe about a dozen soldiers were in attendance.

The Chaplain performed a brief service consisting of prayer, a short bible reading, and a few comments relating to the deceased soldier's sacrifice and the loss to their friends and family. The service lasted only about five minutes.

Memory fails me, but I believe a squad of soldiers fired an honorary salute of three volleys.

The service once again made me reflect on the reasons I was there and the precious things that awaited us at home. My personal feeling of loss was great and surprising to me. I had attended funeral services before, but this was different and had a profound impact.

Yes, the service was brief. We were a group in an exposed area, thus presenting a tempting target for the enemy. We also had work that had to be done. That did not detract from the reverence we wanted to show and the opportunity to share the loss.

SIXTH SENSE

The US Army is perhaps the most effective training organization on earth. The methods may seem slow and cumbersome, however, the knowledge imparted is generally well thought out and provides the basis for mission accomplishment.

As a second lieutenant I had achieved many basic skills through the ROTC program and was further prepared in the Armor Officers Basic Course at Fort Knox, Kentucky. The following nine month tour as a platoon leader in the Second Armored Division at Fort Hood, Texas, provided on hands leadership, maintenance, weaponry, tactics training, and a host of other practical knowledge required to be an effective combat leader.

Upon arrival in South Vietnam and assignment as an armored cavalry platoon leader in Cambodia, it was readily apparent that I had only scratched the surface of required knowledge.

Fortunately, I had my troop commander, platoon sergeant, and combat experienced troopers to help me. Unfortunately, there was not time in the combat situation for me to be coddled and trained. As the platoon commander, my decisions had to be instantaneous and correct. Lives and mission accomplishment were at stake.

Leadership is a multi-faceted thing. Yes, the traits of character, training, and mind-set are important. Equally important is the ability of the leader to focus, plan, and react. While some of these things can be learned, I believe the true leader has to adapt all of the above to his personal character and train his mind to plan and react on what he believes to be the best course of action at the time. Hesitancy leads to failure and in combat failure is not an option.

I slowly discovered that I seemed to be blessed with a sixth sense. I am sure that many people would regard this as an egotistical remark or simply attribute this to an overactive imagination.

There are a number examples of this sixth sense in action. One of which was experienced at our NDP near *Snuol* Cambodia.

It was early in the afternoon and actually was not raining for a change, but of course, the deep-red mud was still everywhere. We had endured several enemy attacks in the location so the site was very reminiscent of battlefield scenes I had seen in the movies. The platoon sergeant and I were talking a few meters behind our vehicles on the perimeter. A LOH (light observation helicopter) had landed about twenty meters behind our position on the perimeter and the occupants of the helicopter had gone to the headquarters track in the center of the NDP.

I remember commenting that I wished the helicopter would soon leave since it was an attractive target and a superb aiming point for enemy gunners. Hardly had the words been spoken when I sensed something odd. I could not see it or consciously hear it, but I was sure it was rifle bullets flying slightly over my head and to my right. I immediately shouted "incoming" several times to alert those around me. As I started running toward my Platoon Leader's track, a heavy barrage of mortar shells and small arms fire erupted all around me. My next move was to hit the mud and low crawl. Adrenaline is a true blessing in a crisis situation. The speed with which I was able to crawl the distance to my track and the way I was able to mount my track, much like a snake going up a tree, will always amaze me. The battle was intense and we were once again successful in repelling a significant enemy force.

After the battle, several of my troopers and the platoon sergeant commented that they were glad to have the early warning and wondered how I knew we were under attack before the heavy fire was placed on us.

It was not long before my troopers began to understand that when I issued words of warning, they should listen. There were many instances when I was able to sense the presence of both manned and unmanned ambushes and many other hazards.

Having given the subject a lot of thought in the years since our service in Southeast Asia, I believe there was nothing mysterious about the so called sixth sense. Yes, there were times when I cannot explain the phenomenon as anything other than divine intervention. But for the majority of cases, I believe it was the constant practice of planning whenever possible, training my mind to be aware of every- thing possible, and practicing awareness to the point where it became a part of my subconscious mind.

Whatever the explanation for the sixth sense, I firmly believe a good combat leader must work to develop his total awareness. I know it can save lives and facilitate mission accomplishment.

THE REAR DOOR

We were deep in the midst of yet another battle. The platoon was positioned behind the berm of the NDP. Heavy fire was being directed at us from the jungle and huge brush piles in front of us. Mortar shells and RPG rounds were numerous and impacting around us and behind us. The small arms fire was heavy but, fortunately, because of our heavy return fire, was not very accurate. The engineers in the center of our NDP were sustaining casualties mostly from the mortar shrapnel.

As was the case in too many battles, many of our vehicle radios were not working properly. Along with the radios that were operating, I had to use arm and hand signals to relay directions to the platoon. We were in a stationary defense, so required communication was minimal. Still, the individual track commanders had to know of any changes or new threats.

The vehicle to my left was a Sheridan tank commanded by a good young sergeant (E-5). That vehicle's radio was as not working properly. For a time, they were firing their machine guns and the main gun. I did notice that they stopped firing the main gun. There was nothing I could do about that at the moment.

Aside from the incoming fire, we were vigilant against the threat of "sappers" sneaking in between our vehicles to detonate explosive charges. Yes, it was a clear day, but in the fog of battle it is almost impossible to guard against everything. There is simply too much going on.

I will never know for sure if I saw something, or merely sensed something was wrong. I thought somebody was edging along the side of my track from front to rear, or in other words from the direction of the enemy.

The ACAV is equipped with a large ramp on the back that is closed when moving or in a battle position. The only access to the inside of the track when the ramp is closed is either by climbing over the top of the track or entering through the rear door or hatch in the back ramp.

I quickly realized someone was attempting to open the rear door. Was it a sapper trying to throw a satchel charge into the vehicle? If that was the case, and he was successful, all of us in the track would likely be killed.

I quickly spun away from my machine gun and drew my .45-caliber pistol. Aiming the pistol at the doorway, a maximum distance of two feet, I moved the pistol safety to the fire position and prepared to shoot. I still did not know who was trying to open the door.

The heavy door swung open quickly and the person who had opened the door was staring at my pistol only a foot or so from his head. It was a difficult situation with only a split second for me to decide what to do. If it were the enemy, he could kill us all almost instantly if I did not shoot him first. If it was not the enemy, I certainly did not want to shoot one of my own troopers.

Thankfully, it was not the enemy. My trooper and I both stood frozen for a few brief seconds. I will never know which one of us was scared the most. I slowly lowered my pistol.

The trooper was the sergeant in command of the Sheridan tank to my left. As indicated before, his radio was not working and he felt it was important that I know he had lost the capability to fire the main gun.

Needless to say, my leadership skills were greatly tested. Here was a good NCO who at great risk to his personal safety, tried to do the right thing by keeping his platoon leader advised of his track's fighting capability. I am sure I said "yelled" some not very nice things and sent him back to his track before I returned to doing my job.

Once again, this entire scenario occurred in a very short time span of a minute or less. Sometimes you have to react the best you can.

I do remember that I sought him out after the battle and we talked about the situation.

It was important to me that he understood what he had done so he could learn from the experience. I also told him the truth: that he was a good soldier and leader and a valuable member of the platoon. I also remember telling him that I was just as scared as he was.

WOUNDED

In spite of all our technology and no matter how hard we try, it is a given that casualties are a part of war.

In Southeast Asia we considered ourselves very fortunate compared to our predecessors in WWII and The Korean War. Although we too experienced heavy combat, our equipment, protective gear, and support systems were much advanced. Our likelihood of experiencing casualties was lessened and perhaps most significantly our medical support systems were far advanced as compared to those of our predecessors.

When we had wounded, the first line of defense was our medics. No they were not doctors. They were well trained in first aid techniques and for the most part were brave young men who would do whatever it took to reach and treat the wounded even in the heat of battle.

In previous wars the wounded were evacuated to crude field hospitals, state of the art at that time, either by foot or ground vehicle. That process could easily require hours or even days.

I believe our most important asset for the care of wounded was the availability of helicopters. When someone was wounded, we would immediately call for a medivac (medical evacuation helicopter). It was seldom more than twenty minutes before the helicopter arrived. If a medevac helicopter was not readily available, the nearest Huey would almost always come to pick up the wounded.

The process could be difficult. If it were in a period of darkness, rain, or if we were experiencing enemy fire, it made no difference.

The brave pilots and crew members of those helicopters would face almost any condition to reach the wounded. They knew that speedy evacuation saved lives. Besides, that is what American soldiers do when an American soldier or allied soldier is in trouble. They find a way to help.

The crewmen on the helicopters, sometimes medics, would continue efforts to stabilize the wounded soldiers. The pilots would fly as quickly as possible to the nearest field hospital.

The result of the quick evacuations and advanced medical aid available at the field hospitals, was that many soldiers were saved who otherwise would have succumbed to what were often violent wounds.

The loss of our fellow soldiers because of wounds was always devastating to us. We were their friends and had experienced many difficult times with them. Had I known then the things I know now, I would have shared a lot of hugs and sought more laughter.

MIRED VEHICLES

The Cambodian jungle was a beautiful and interesting place. Unfortunately, its beautiful trees, both natural jungle and rubber plantations, occasional rice paddies, swamp areas, and soft earth made it a somewhat inhospitable and dangerous area for us to conduct our search-and-destroy missions. The enemy had plenty of places to hide in ambush and the terrain often made it difficult for us to maneuver.

We had spent the day conducting our search-and-destroy mission somewhere east of *Snuol* and not far from the Cambodian and South Vietnam border. We were approximately ten kilometers from our troop NDP and to my knowledge any friendly troops. It was growing late and we were anxious to complete our mission and return to the relative safety of our troop NDP. At least there we would be close to friendly troops.

We had encountered the enemy on several occasions during the day and were running a little low on ammunition. Resupply in the dense jungle surrounding us was not an option. Not a big problem as long as we did not get involved in a significant firefight.

As we prepared to search and clear the last area of the day, disaster struck. We were on the edge of a marshy area about seventy-five yards across and a few hundred yards long. One of our ACAVs become deeply mired in the mud. Obviously, it would take some time to retrieve the vehicle.

In view of the vulnerable position of the mired ACAV, I had little choice other than to place the majority of the platoon in a herringbone formation for three hundred and sixty degree security. Two

ACAVs attempted to work their way to the far side of the clearing to provide flank security for the mired vehicle. One vehicle made the trip safely, but of course, the second vehicle became deeply mired close to the other side of the clearing.

It was readily apparent that we would not be able to retrieve the vehicles before darkness. I immediately informed the troop commander via radio of our situation. While the crew went to work to extract the mired vehicles, I preplanned artillery fires and selected a small area with relatively solid ground where we could form a platoon NDP and wait for morning. That was a good plan in the situation, but of course, it required getting the mired vehicles operational again.

Our position was precarious. We were spread out and widely separated from possible support troops. At least two of our vehicles had relatively unprotected flanks and I had men working in the open. Of course, the enemy knew where we were. Armored platoons are noisy and have little stealth capability. In view of our previous contacts during the day, we knew the enemy was nearby. There was little doubt in my mind that we were being watched.

As feared, darkness soon set in. All platoon members not actively working to free the mired vehicles were on 100 percent alert. No one thought about sleep. We all knew the seriousness of the situation and we all knew we were the only possible protection for the troopers working in the open terrain.

It would be reasonable to wonder how I allowed my unit to get into such a situation. While I was undoubtedly responsible for all that my unit did or failed to do, I also understand that conditions are sometimes beyond our control. We sometimes have to simply take the necessary actions to make whatever situation in which we are immersed, workable to our advantage if possible. If not possible, we minimize the damage and move forward.

The darkness made the work to free the mired vehicles much slower and more dangerous. Before long, the troop commander informed me that our squadron commander had requested support from air force flare ships and they would be arriving soon.

The flare ships soon arrived and turned the absolute darkness into brilliant daylight. The flares were very powerful and were deployed on parachutes at a relatively high altitude. If one flare was used up or drifted away, another was deployed in time to keep the high visibility throughout the process.

The flares gave us the distinct advantage of good visibility both to perform the heavy and dangerous work of retrieving the mired ACAVs and also provided good vision to our troopers who were guarding against enemy activity.

As in most things in life, there is a flip side to the use of such flares. Bottom line, if we could clearly see the enemy, he could clearly see us. My biggest fear was a sniper attack on my troopers working in the open.

All things considered, the advantages of the flares far outweighed the disadvantages in our situation. It was still a nerve racking time.

After an hour or so of working by the light of the flares, our vehicles were freed and assembled in a platoon formation once again.

We immediately moved to the site I had selected earlier and establish our platoon NDP. All personnel remained on 50 percent alert through the night. That meant that at least half of each crew was on guard duty rather than the normal one trooper per vehicle. We all knew we were very vulnerable to attack that night and could hope for help only from artillery fires and helicopter gunships.

I, of course, reported our situation to the troop commander. He agreed that I should remain in my current position rather than attempt to return to the troop NDP that night. He added, to my surprise, that he wanted to congratulate my platoon on a job well done that day. He noted that he knew it had been a rough day and that we had overcome all the obstacles required to accomplish the mission. I, of course, passed his praise on to the platoon.

Fortunately, the remainder of the night was uneventful.

Shortly before daylight, I received a new mission from the troop commander. We were ordered to extend our search a little farther to the east.

Before we moved out, I reminded all the track commanders that we needed to conserve ammunition. I will never know why, but no resupply helicopter was scheduled for us that day. I am sure there was a good reason, but we still had to deal with the situation.

We did not come into contact with enemy forces that day, but prudently expended some ammunition in reconnaissance by fire. Reconnaissance by fire was a method entailing shooting into suspected ambush sites, for example, to either destroy the ambushing force or force them to return fire before we were in their killing zone. Surprise in combat is a great asset only if friendly troops are doing the surprising.

Late in the afternoon, we had completed our mission. We encountered a sister squadron's NDP and stopped to see if we could arrange to borrow enough ammunition to ensure we could finish our journey with some measure of safety. To my chagrin, the answer was no. That was the only time I ever witnessed fellow GIs fail to do whatever they could to help other GIs in trouble.

Many years later I encountered the officer who had denied us. He did not remember me or the incident. I suppose I should be ashamed to admit it, but I left him with no doubt that I felt he was the lowest of life forms and not deserving of the uniform. Didn't do any good, but I think I felt better.

Darkness was approaching and we had a long way to go down the jungle road to our troop NDP. A thunderstorm was approaching and I knew that would affect our visibility and limit the possibility of gunship support if we got in trouble.

I ordered our vehicle commanders to drive as fast as possible. This was done for three reasons. First, if we drove fast enough, any mines we hit would, hopefully, explode behind the vehicle. Secondly, I hoped to surprise any ambush personnel and be past them before they could spring their trap. This was necessary because of our low-ammunition supply. Third, I wanted to reach our troop NDP before total darkness. The dangers of moving at night were extreme.

Fortunately, we arrived at the troop NDP without further incident and after refueling took our positions on the perimeter. I really believe, the troop commander was as glad to see us as were glad to see him. He knew the previous couple of days had been an exceptionally difficult series of missions.

THE LETTER

We had been conducting operations in Cambodia for several weeks.

After a long day on a search-and-destroy mission we returned to our filthy, muddy, and wet NDP. If felt like we were home for the evening.

As I suppose happens in most if not all combat situations, it took a long time for my mail to find me. "Joy oh joy!" Mail call had my first bundle of letters. I was so happy to finally have a tangible connection with my loved ones at home. I was tired of being lonely.

I clearly remember sorting several envelopes by the date they were mailed. The first was about a month old and I tore into it like a Christmas package. It was from my dad and I was thrilled. He wrote that the family was doing well and looking forward to my return home.

The tone of the letter and my mood changed instantly. He wrote that one of my very best friends had been killed in a train wreck shortly after I shipped out to Asia. He had just completed a tour in the US Air Force and had a new job working for the railroad. I could barely comprehend the news. We had been close friends since about the sixth grade. I had not the experience to cope with the tragedy. After all, I was the one that was supposed to be in harm's way. It just wasn't fair.

I knew I really needed a friend to help me work through my sense of loss. Of course, I could not show what might be perceived as weakness or burden any of my platoon members.

I soon heard that a fellow platoon leader and friend from our days at Fort Hood had just led his platoon into the NDP. I waited a few minutes to give him time to settle his platoon in for the night before going to his position.

When I arrived at his position I was shocked to see him sitting beside his command track with his head lowered into his hands. He was weeping and obviously greatly troubled.

I spoke to him and he seemed genuinely glad to see me. It seems he needed to talk to a friend as much or more than I did.

The story was soon revealed. He had been on an extended search-and-destroy mission. One of his tracks had hit a large mine, resulting in the death of two of his troopers. I tried to understand and comfort him as much as my inexperience would allow. We talked until I had to return to my platoon area for the night. I knew he was not in a position to help me, so I did not mention the death of my dear friend.

We were young but aging quickly. What a way to learn how to navigate through the tough realities of life.

THE AVLB

It was late May and our platoon was still conducting patrols in the area of *Snuol*, Cambodia. The jungle was dense and the few roads were mere trails. The occasional village would typically be on the edge of a rice paddy only a few hundred square yards in size. It was apparently enough to feed the primitive villagers.

We received orders to begin the return to the S. Vietnamese border, thus ending we thought, our ordeal in Cambodia.

Murphy was right again. If it could go wrong, it would.

As the majority of US troops began the retrograde operation, I was notified that my platoon was to defend and extract an AVLB that had become seriously mired in a rice paddy outside of one of the villages. It happened to be the village with which we had experienced the most interaction and, I believe, gained the trust and support of the villagers whom we had attempted to help.

We soon began the recovery efforts to extract the AVLB. Unfortunately, the AVLB was sunken deeply and the flat bottom of the nearly sixty-ton chassis was in the grasp of enormous suction by the mud at the bottom of the rice paddy.

Recognizing that we were well equipped with equipment, technology, and training, we felt the task at hand was a simple one. Wrong!

We tried many different methods to get the AVLB moving. We secured a tank retriever, a huge tank like wrecker made just for such situations. We used to say the tank retriever was fuel efficient since it got about eight gallons to the mile when traveling. Even that monster could not accomplish the job.

We soon requested and were supplied an additional tank retriever. We hitched the two retrievers together and pulled without success. Our next step was to dig under the AVLB and place C-4 explosive to break the suction of the mud. As we exploded the C-4, the two tank retrievers were pulling with all their magnificent power. Same result, still stuck in the mud.

The situation was becoming very serious. In view of the general pullback, my platoon was alone in a heavily enemy infested area. Our only real support in case of attack, would be limited helicopter gunships, not very practical at night, and long range artillery. To my knowledge, we were the furthermost West of any US forces in Cambodia.

We had spent about two days and two nights attempting to extract the AVLB. In desperation, we exploded more C-4 and hooked our three Sheridan Tanks in tandem with the tank retrievers for one last try. It did not work.

It was late in the morning when I advised my troop commander that we had expended all options we could muster and requested advice and direction. As I awaited a response, he apparently was coordinating with his commander. It was with amazement that I learned how we were finally successful.

The local villagers were either tired of us tearing up their rice paddy or sincerely wanted to help. They asked, through our interpreter, if they could try to free the vehicle. Their offer seemed ridiculous in view of their lack of technology, but I had nothing to lose, so I agreed. We were waiting for further orders anyway.

It was a slow time, so I watched as the villagers started to work. It required about an hour for them to gather a large number of bamboo poles and shove them through the loose mud to a position under the vehicle. Essentially, they built a raft.

The village chief soon began motioning the crew to start moving the AVLB. With the help of one tank retriever, the AVLB was almost immediately freed from the muddy death grip of the rice paddy.

We were all amazed. The simple people of the village had accomplished in short order what all our mighty equipment and technology could not.

I will never be sure, but I believe the bamboo provided enough lift to break the suction of the mud on the chassis and as the AVLB began to move, provided some traction.

The troop commander was, of course, immediately notified. He ordered us to escort the AVLB and tank retrievers to his position. That was probably the sweetest order I ever received.

We quickly thanked the villagers, probably gave them some MREs as a thank you, and prepared to move out.

We made very good time, everyone knew we were still in great danger. It was with great relief that we reached our troop NDP late in the evening.

JUNGLE NAVIGATION

The requirements for knowing where you are, where you are going, and how to get there are critical in a combat theater. You have to be able to correctly report your position to keep higher headquarters informed, to request supporting artillery and air support. If you are asking for heavy artillery support, it is a good idea not to have them fire on your position because you did not correctly tell them where you were. Obviously the same principle applies for other types of support and coordination with friendly troops.

I was able to take comfort in my navigation skills. Generally, all we had to work with were a map and compass. In dense forest, it is often impossible to identify landmarks. It is also very difficult to judge distance when you can only see twenty or thirty feet. Jungle navigation is much like night navigation. You just can't see anything. Add to these difficulties the facts that you are constantly moving and have all the normal distractions of directing a combat unit.

Allow me to digress a moment to explain why I was generally comfortable with my map-reading skills. Of course, my training, both classroom and live practice, had taught me a lot. I tended, however, to take navigation more seriously than many of my contemporaries.

During my time as an armored cavalry platoon leader at Fort Hood, Texas, I experienced navigation in many types of terrain, including, but not limited to, hills, wetlands, forest, and plains. On a particular annual test, our platoon was required to attack for approximately thirty miles across all types of terrain. The exercise lasted three days and three nights. I was followed closely by a US Army Captain who was evaluating our performance.

On the third morning, after three nights without sleep, we were all exhausted. The evaluator approached me and, to my great delight, informed me that we had obtained a perfect score to that point. He then gave me instructions for the final portion of the test. We were to attack and seize a hill a few kilometers away. To initiate the attack, we traveled through a small river, over several ridgelines, and through a lot of dense foliage. Upon reaching our objective, I ordered the platoon to attack. All seemed to go well. As the evaluator approached me, I was filled with a feeling of relief knowing we had performed superbly. The evaluator informed me that we had done well, except that it would have been better for us to have attacked the correct hill. He graciously let us try again. That wasn't too disastrous in an exercise. In a combat zone, remember, there are no do-overs. I swore to myself that I would do everything in my power to learn to be a great land navigator. My efforts were successful.

In the jungle environment, I used the available tools. I would use the compass and the odometer of my vehicle to estimate distance and direction traveled. If I felt I needed verification, I would ask the troop commander to fire a flare from a known position, allowing me to do a back azimuth. Sometimes, I could ask a nearby helicopter to verify my position from his high vantage point. I almost always knew exactly where my unit was located.

There were instances where others challenged the correctness of my reported position. If they were correct, I was appreciative. They were seldom correct. In one such instance, I was deep in the jungle. The Squadron Executive officer informed me via radio that I needed to verify my position. I did so, and he angrily told me that I was at least three kilometers from that position. I knew that was impossible, but he out ranked me. In desperation, I asked him to give me my position coordinates as he believed them to be. Upon checking my map, I saw that position was on the far side of the Saigon River. I certainly did not recall having taken my unit for a deep water swim that morning. Fortunately, I was once again saved by the Squadron Commander. He in no uncertain terms told the Executive Officer that I was where I said I was, that he should figure out where he (expletive) was, and he *would stop* harassing me.

Such were the rigors of jungle navigation. The wise leader does everything possible to hone his navigation skills.

LEAVING CAMBODIA

I had long been familiar with the old saying that the best view of some places is the one in your rearview mirror. Never before had the words been so true to me.

Cambodia is truly a beautiful country. The jungle and the people were truly amazing to experience firsthand. Unfortunately, we were not in country for a sightseeing tour. Our business was war and business was good.

In just a few weeks I had changed from an eager young cavalry officer to a battle hardened and, hopefully, wiser leader of combat troops. I could not at the time see all the changes but they had occurred.

Our platoon and troop had made a difference. In spite of huge obstacles and the sorrow that comes with combat, we had accomplished our missions large and small. I knew at the time that I had earned the confidence of my superiors and more importantly that of my troopers. This was important because we could expect many more challenges when we returned to S. Vietnam.

We received our orders to be the trailing platoon as the squadron began its journey down the long dusty roads through the jungle. We were essentially the rear guard and were most likely to be attacked.

As we neared the border of S. Vietnam, I received new orders. The squadron column was halted and my platoon proceeded to move into the lead position of the column. I was told later by my troop commander that they expected an ambush at or near the border as we returned. The squadron commander said he wanted his most reliable platoon to encounter and disrupt any ambush. An honor it was, but it was a dubious honor in our eyes.

As we approached the border we saw a sign mounted on two metal poles. It simply said "Welcome to Vietnam." A continuous cheer arose as we drove passed the sign. We were happy to put Cambodia behind us.

We were told that we would spend the night at a major installation not far from Nui Ba Den. Nui Ba Den, roughly translated as "Black Virgin Mountain," was a small singular mountain that rose out of many miles of flat plains. It held little significance for us except that we knew many fierce battles had been fought for control of the mountain. Apparently the US troops held the top of the mountain as an observation post while the remainder of the mountain was in control of the VC. A strange and tenuous situation for the GIs on top of the mountain.

We were thrilled to learn that we would spend the night at a major installation. That would mean no guard duty, showers, visits to officer and enlisted clubs, and maybe even a trip to the post exchange. "Wrong!" When we arrived, we were directed into a large fenced parking lot, which was roomy enough to park the entire squadron. We saw that local military police were posted at all possible exits. It was disappointing, but I also understood the local commander probably feared trouble from our troopers wanting to unwind. No doubt his fears were well grounded.

I never returned to Cambodia, but I didn't leave anything there worth going back to retrieve.

I often have thought of the Cambodian people. They were good people who had to endure the horrors of the Khmer Rouge in later years. All they wanted to do was live their lives their way and in peace. I have to control my anger when someone criticizes troops who fight for freedom around the world. It may not be our country but it is our world. I know the value of giving for the right thing. If we don't do what is necessary, who will?

THE LOST ROAD

It was the second day in Vietnam after leaving Cambodia. Our squadron was headed generally southeast to an area Northwest of Saigon. We were traveling fast in a single file convoy encompassing the entire squadron. My platoon was in the lead. The convoy was several miles in length because of our need to maintain combat intervals of about one hundred feet between tracks.

The day was hot but not unbearable. Our speed provided a good breeze as we traveled the long asphalt road. We, of course, slowed our rate of speed as we passed through various towns and villages. The locals were smart enough to yield to our massive convoy. Their mopeds and buses would have been no match for our steel behemoths.

I enjoyed passing through the towns. They were crude by our standards but were bustling with commerce and locals carrying out their daily routines. I had never seen anything quite like them.

Late in the afternoon I received a directive to turn left at a paved road a few kilometers ahead of my position. I located the position of the intersection on my map and advised my lead track commander of the directive. I had my driver relay the current speedometer reading on my track as a reference point to help in locating the intersection.

As we approached the intersection, the landscape was very strange. It had once been forested, but now because of deforestation spraying, all the vegetation was dead and appeared to be only brush a few feet high. One could see for miles, but there was really nothing to see and certainly no landmarks I could use for navigation.

In twenty or thirty minutes we reached the point where I thought the intersection should be located. We could not see any roads other than the main highway on which we were traveling. I used the radio to confer with my lead track commander and my platoon sergeant. All agreed we should be at the intersection.

I sent two or three tracks another mile down the road to see if they could find our objective. They found nothing. This was very troublesome. We were professional combat scouts and should be more than capable of finding something as obvious as a road.

There was nothing else I could do to find the road intersection. I radioed the troop commander that we were unable to find the road and apprised him of the actions we had taken. As we talked, the squadron commander came on the troop net and informed me rather gruffly that he was aloft in his command helicopter and would soon be there to help me find the road. The situation was embarrassing to me, but the mission was more important than my personal pride.

The squadron commander soon arrived above my position and flew back and forth for a few minutes. He could not locate the road either. He directed me to pull of the highway at my current location and clear the way for a squadron NDP.

Later that evening, as we provided security for the squadron NDP, the troop commander called me to his location. This was not unusual but I was apprehensive.

Upon meeting him, I found him to be laughing heartily. The missing road mystery had been solved.

The situation had been escalated to higher headquarters. They learned that the road had been missing for several years and the maps were not updated. It seems that when the asphalt road had been abandoned, the locals had dug up the asphalt by hand and carried it home to pave around their hootches. Weather, nonuse, and new underbrush had erased all traces of the road. I was off the hook, but realized I still had a lot to learn about this strange war.

INDIGENOUS PEOPLE

Although there were several groups of people inhabiting the various areas I worked in, my experiences were primarily with rural Cambodians and both rural and urban South Vietnamese.

Please note that I did my best to keep distance between my troopers and the locals in many instances. This was not due to an elitist attitude. The hard facts were that we could not tell by looking which ones were our enemies and which ones were either allies or simply neutral just wanting to live their lives in peace.

The Cambodian people, as mentioned elsewhere, were extremely primitive in our view. They were at first fearful of us, but with time and effort we were able to show them that our sole interest was in eliminating the VC and NVA forces. I believe our actions showed that we would help them where we could.

The Cambodians soon earned my respect. They were a proud people and in my view a giving people. They had little, but clearly were family and village oriented and did what little they could to help us. It was obvious the VC ruled them with fear rather than caring.

A little sideline comment. The Cambodians I saw in South Vietnam generally were descendants of French plantation owners and Vietnamese mothers. They were generally physically attractive and certainly larger in physical structure than the normal Vietnamese.

The South Vietnamese people were generally thin and small in stature. I have always believed this was indicative of diet and customs. A large part, I suspect was the fact that their country had been at war for many years. It is hard to prosper and have a truly nutritious diet in those circumstances.

I had only limited contact with the urban population. The cities were crowded and often smelled terrible. This could be attributed to the lack of proper sanitation systems and the hot humid weather. The traffic was incredible and seemed to be ruled by the law of everyone has the right of way. The mopeds were plentiful and would weave in and out at their discretion. Good luck to anyone trying to walk across a main thoroughfare.

The nature of our business kept us primarily in the countryside. We had some contact with villagers and, of course, the seemingly ever present "short time girls." It seemed odd to me, but I do not ever remember seeing a single farmhouse. They were all in small villages. This probably had a lot to do with the need for community and defense.

The average village consisted of about ten to twenty huts with a dirt road through the middle of the village. The huts were made of whatever materials they could obtain and lacked windows or doors. There was obviously a total absence of running water, sewers, and electricity. It was not uncommon to see the outer walls covered in flattened beer cans. I assume this was the best they could do for siding. Some had a makeshift shower on the outside for bathing. They did not seem to care who saw them bathing.

Perhaps the scene can best be related through the following experience. I was ordered to place my platoon at both ends of a very small village for the night. I never knew the reason for this mission. The night was uneventful and as morning dawned I was struck by the surprising beauty. The sun rose over the rice paddies and the rustic village reminded me of something I saw as a boy in the National Geographic magazine.

I ensured my troopers were awake and we all reached for our morning rations in preparation for the day. My mood soon changed. As the villagers arose their first order of business seemed to be a trip to the outhouse. The problem was that they did not have outhouses. They all moved to the middle of the road and proceeded to take care of their personal business. There is nothing quite like the sight of twenty or thirty men women and children using the restroom in front of you to ruin your appetite. I chose to forget about breakfast that morning.

Perhaps the following story will better illustrate our dilemma of not knowing who to trust. We were somewhere about fifteen miles west of the Regimental base camp at Dian. Our troop was escorting the squadron headquarters to establish a new squadron NDP just outside of a small village. Our route took us through the village on the dusty dirt road. As we slowly passed through, the villagers all came out to watch. Most were silent but we soon got an idea of our welcome. An older lady began screaming at us in Vietnamese and menacingly waved at butcher knife at us. Of course, we were not afraid of her but we knew this was a bad sign. At one point we came to a stop while we waited for the tracks ahead of us to maneuver into the new NDP site. I noticed an older man apparently listening to a portable civilian radio perched on his shoulder. This did not seem quite right to me. It soon became obvious that he was talking to the radio. He must have been transmitting to the VC the information on the armored column he was observing. I ordered a few troopers to dismount and take him into custody. Before they could reach him he disappeared into a hut. To this day, I do not know where he hid. There must have been a tunnel we could not locate for I know we would have seen him if he had left the hut in any other way. Welcome to the friendly neighborhood.

As our troops entered the NDP area, a one-armed teenage girl was taken into custody. She had been walking around the area dropping small homemade explosive devices.

It was sad, but this is what we had to deal with anytime we were near the local people.

I have since known a number of Vietnamese immigrants who were so fortunate as to find new lives in the United States. I find them to be friendly and hardworking people who appreciate their freedoms and want to live good peaceful lives.

Living in a war torn country makes a difference.

AUTOMATIC AMBUSH

Few soldiers I know would describe war as anything less than a dirty business. Whatever the mission may be, it almost always incorporates the need to deny the enemy of something and to inflict maximum casualties on the enemy. Numerous devices are used to achieve the desired results ranging from the most highly technical to the crudest devices.

The battles in Southeast Asia were often waged against an unseen enemy without the benefit of clear battle lines. The jungle, rice paddies, rubber plantations, and mountains provided significant concealment for the elusive enemy. It seemed he was like Santa Claus, he was everywhere.

Our troopers and foot soldiers were constantly on the alert for booby traps. They were easily concealed and could be of almost any nature. They ranged from unexploded bombs and artillery shells to simple wooden stakes hidden in the foliage. The common denominator was that they were all potentially lethal.

The enemy was not alone in their ability to devise booby traps. Long before I arrived in the combat theater, some ingenious GIs had devised one of the deadliest. We called it the Automatic Ambush (AA). Some units called them Mechanical Ambushes.

It was virtually impossible to always observe enemy trails and avenues of approach. The AA was a good answer to this problem.

The AA was simple in nature. It required a piece of fishing line a few feet in length, a battery, a clothes pin, a plastic spoon, two thumb tacks, a wooden stake or small tree limb, a few feet of electrical wire, and a claymore mine.

Upon selecting a site to set the ambush, normally along a trail, it would be deployed by one trooper being overwatched for security by others. The security force would maintain a healthy distance just in case of premature detonation of the AA. Troopers normally took turns at this hazardous task, but some of the seasoned troopers would insist on the duty since they were well experienced.

Both thumb tacks would be placed inside the jaws of the clothespin with the sharp ends pointing out to ensure that when the clothespin was closed, the heads of the thumb tacks would contact. The electrical lead wire to the claymore mine was secured under the head of one thumb tack and the electrical lead to the battery was secured under the head of the other thumb tack. The clothespin would be attached to the wooden stake or small tree about six inches to a foot off the ground. The fishing line (tripwire) would be tied to a small bush and stretched across the path expected to be taken by the enemy. The other end of the tripwire would be securely tied to a small hole in the handle of the plastic spoon. The claymore mine would be placed facing the anticipated path of the enemy. The plastic spoon would be placed in the jaws of the clothespin thus acting as an insulator between the two thumb tacks. Great care was taken to ensure the apparatus was well camouflaged. The last step was to attach the electrical wire to the battery placed a safe distance from the apparatus.

The theory was simple and effective. When the enemy soldier stumbled into the trip wire, it would pull the plastic spoon from between the jaws of the clothespin. As the heads of the thumbtacks made contact, the circuit between the battery would be completed resulting in detonation of the claymore mine.

Of course AAs were not always successful. When we left an area of operations, we always retrieved any unexploded AAs. To leave them there would pose an obvious hazard to future allied troops and civilians.

Retrieving the AAs required strict adherence to two basic rules. First, the trooper who set the AA was always the trooper who retrieved the AA. He would know better than anyone where the components were located. Remember they were well camouflaged. This practice reduced the risk of accidental detonation. Claymore mines are inanimate objects and don't care who they kill.

The second rule of retrieving AAs is to assume the enemy has found and moved them. It seldom happened but there were instances where the enemy had successfully dismantled the device. If so, they could have either taken the components with them or relocated the AA to endanger our troops when we came to retrieve it. Retrieving the AAs was not a fun task.

The enemy was wily and would sometimes use dogs to precede them as they moved along trails. The intent was for the dogs to hit the tripwire thus allowing the enemy to be clear of the explosion.

My first experience with an AA came the first night after joining L Troop in the Cambodian Jungle. Sometime, I believe a few hours after midnight, we heard a loud explosion a few hundred yards from our NDP. My concerns were allayed when a trooper told me one of our AAs had been triggered and we could check the site after daylight.

Early the following morning, the platoon moved to check the site of the exploded AA. We found the ambush had been successful. One enemy body lay in the middle of the trail. After establishing a secure perimeter, the troopers began inspecting the site.

The first action was to check the enemy corpse for booby traps. One trooper got a rope and grappling hook from one of the tracks and used the grappling hook to turn the body over to ensure no grenades or other devices had been placed under the body. When it was determined to be safe, the clothing was checked for documents that might be of intelligence value.

This was the first enemy casualty I had encountered. To my surprise, it did not bother me. My mind quickly adapted, as a self defense mechanism I think, to regard deceased enemy soldiers as a non entity. It never worked that way for our soldiers.

Investigation of the area revealed evidence indicating the enemy soldier had not been alone. We broadened the search and soon discovered a hastily dug and covered shallow grave containing the bodies of several enemy soldiers. The grave, of course, had to be opened, bodies counted, and any documents checked for intelligence value. This was not a pleasant task. This young lieutenant was learning more and more of the lessons related to combat.

The AAs were an important part of our arsenal. They denied or slowed enemy access, inflicted casualties on the enemy, and I am sure made the enemy very nervous as they attempted movements in our area of operations. All this was accomplished with minimal risk to our troops.

AUTOMATIC AMBUSH BATTERIES

The need for proper supplies in war is obviously critical. Everyone can easily understand the importance of "beans and bullets" for without them the soldier can neither survive nor fight. Often it is the lesser recognized supplies that can play a critical role.

One of the primary elements required to deploy automatic ambushes is the common lantern battery. Without it, there is no power source to detonate the explosives when the trip wire is moved.

Our troop had reached a point where we had a serious shortage of the required batteries. The troop commander called me and one of the other platoon leaders to the command post and ordered us to catch the next helicopter to Bien Hoa AFB. Our mission was to acquire the needed batteries. Since one lieutenant should have been able to accomplish the mission, I was sure the trip was a reward to let two battle weary lieutenants have a small break from the daily routine.

The lieutenant who accompanied me was a good friend for whom I had the utmost respect. He was a West Point graduate and later achieved the rank of Major General. I have no doubt that he earned the position.

The fact that my friend was a West Point graduate was a primary factor in his assignment to this mission. One of his classmates was the personal aide to the commanding general of a Signal Corps brigade located at Bien Hoa. Guess what! The signal corps has access to lots of batteries.

We boarded the chopper (helicopter) early in the morning and arrived at Bien Hoa AFB in about thirty minutes.

Bien Hoa was an established base with paved streets and many temporary buildings. It was hard to distinguish the difference between the base and those we would see in the United States. If we had not known we were in Vietnam, we would probably have wondered just exactly where we were. Definitely a change to our accustomed environment in the field.

Our personal appearance did not exactly fit in. We had not seen a shower in months, and our uniforms were dirty and ragged. At first we were a little self-conscious but soon realized we were the combat troops that the others we saw were there to support. In this case, clothes definitely did not make the man.

We found the lieutenant at the Signal Corps Brigade. The two friends chatted for a while as I listened. I didn't mind for there was no threat of somebody shooting at us. This was also the first time they had met and were able to share the loss of a classmate who had been killed by a booby trap a few weeks earlier. My friend was there when the classmate was killed and I could see that it was a great loss to him. I think the chance to talk about the loss of their common friend helped them both.

After a short time, the Signal Corps lieutenant invited us to lunch at the commanding general's (General Abrams) mess. As we entered the mess we were both in nothing less than a state of shock. We were greeted by a lovely Vietnamese hostess in a long and beautiful oriental dress. The floors were carpeted, and I believe the lighting was chandeliers. The tables were draped in nice white table cloths and set with beautiful dinnerware. There were more pieces of silver at each setting than I have ever seen in any other restaurant.

We soon noticed looks of disdain from many of the officers, young and old, seated at the tables. I am sure it was our ragged and dirty appearance. We felt somewhat out of place, but did not let it bother us much. Who were they to look down on us when they lived in such relative comfort while our troops struggled to survive in the poorest of conditions?

A well dressed waiter soon appeared to take our orders. We were told to ask for anything we wanted. We thought about ordering steaks, but chose hamburgers instead. I think we were still too intimidated to attempt a full meal. After all, how were we supposed to know which pieces of silverware to use? Not exactly a place for our fingers or plastic spoons and a canteen cup. I think we also felt some guilt that we had access to such finery while our troopers did not.

After the meal, the signal corps lieutenant asks if we would like to see his commanding general's quarters. We thought the invitation was a little odd, but indicated we would. A short walk took us to a row of nice one bedroom houses. The neighborhood looked much like one in a middle income area back home. The houses were not fancy but had a full bathroom, kitchenette, bedroom, and living room. Not exactly like the four men in a tracked vehicle that was our normal abode.

To be fair, I am sure the men and officers at the base were mostly soldiers just doing their best to accomplish mission. It was simply the luck of the draw that they were assigned to positions with what I considered to be outstanding living conditions. If, as we imagined, some of them looked at us unfavorably, then it was good that they were not in the field. That kind is not worthy of our troopers.

It was nearing mid-afternoon and time for us to return to the field. The cases of batteries were loaded on a chopper for us and we expressed our thanks and goodbyes.

The ride back to the NDP was uneventful and the batteries were disseminated to the various vehicle crew.

I think we were both grateful for the break, but were more than happy to be back with our troops where we felt we belonged.

C-4

C-4 explosives were a mainstay of our daily operations. For the farm boys it was like bailing wire in that it could be used to fix almost anything, or so it seemed. Once again, I am talking about actual uses, which may or may not be the uses intended by army regulations.

C-4 is a white malleable plastic explosive compound similar in appearance and texture to play-dough. It can easily be separated into smaller pieces or mashed together into larger pieces and can be shaped to conform to almost any object.

It is very safe to handle and requires a detonation source, usually a blasting cap, to render it into an effective explosive. To use the C-4 as an explosive, we would place a blasting cap into the lump of C-4. A wire would be run to a safe location from which we would initiate the blast by crossing the terminals of a nine volt battery or using what we called a "clacker." The battery or clacker would provide an electric charge to ignite the blasting cap, which in turn caused the C-4 to explode.

The intended uses were for clearing stumps, creating obstacles, destroying bridges, or any of a large variety of military missions requiring explosives.

One of the worst abuses I recall came on a hot afternoon on the edge of a large rice paddy. As I walked along the perimeter, I noticed one of the ACAV crew working on an armored fender that had somehow been forced inward and was in danger of interfering with the operation of the track. I paid little heed as they were a good crew and presumed capable of doing their maintenance work. Suddenly I heard a loud explosion and saw a large piece of heavy metal, approximately one foot by two foot, flying high into the air and out into the jungle. After assuring myself that we were not under attack, it only took a moment to realize what had happened. The armored fender was nearly one inch thick and very sturdy. Failing the use of heavy hammers, pry bars etc., the crew had placed what they believed to be just the right amount of C-4 behind the fender thinking the force of the explosion would straighten the fender. Obviously they had miscalculated the amount of C-4 required. Fortunately, no one was killed by the flying metal and the fender would no longer interfere with the vehicle track. I did not even talk to the crew about it. They knew not to do that again.

Another popular use of C-4 was to light a small piece and use it just as we would use a can of Sterno today. When lit with a match, the C-4 would not explode and would provide a small hot flame sufficient to heat a ration meal or a canteen cup of water in which we could make instant coffee or hot chocolate.

CLEANING THE MACHINE GUN

As mentioned before, combat is not always an active endeavor. There are times when the soldier is not on a patrol, in a firefight, or otherwise engaged. In his off time he writes letters, reads, daydreams of being home, or is maintaining his equipment.

In view of the fact that I needed to set a good example, I began cleaning my M60 machine gun. It wasn't easy in the mud, but it had to be done.

I have never been mechanically inclined and it was quite evident that I was struggling somewhat.

Suddenly a voice came from over my shoulder. It was a young specialist who manned the machine gun on my right rear in the APC. He was a quiet young man from the Deep South. He did not seem to have had much formal education. He was always respectful and did his best to be a good soldier.

It was a surprise to hear his next words. He asked if he could clean the machine gun for me. I thanked him and added that it was my responsibility to care for my assigned weapon, and that he in essence did not need to do my work for me.

His answer to me was eye opening and provided yet another profound lesson learned.

His response went something like this. "Sir, I know you want to do your job. Please understand that when we are in a firefight, we stand side by side or back to back. Sir, you have my back. I need to know that your machine gun is going to work like it should."

It did not take much thought to understand what he was saying. I never again attempted to clean my machine gun. Because of his efforts, it was always in good working order.

The lesson learned, or at least reinforced, is that no one can be everything. We have to learn to rely on those around us, especially in combat. I will ever be grateful to that young specialist.

HELICOPTER DOWN

The afternoon was sunny and dry with a light breeze and generally pleasant. It was one of the rare days when we were providing security for the L Troop NDP rather than patrolling in the surrounding area.

The NDP was established behind the berm the engineers had constructed and looked out into the jungle. The main road ran just outside of the NDP area.

We were resting, cleaning weapons, writing letters and enjoying the then peaceful day.

The voice on the radio told me to report to the troop commander immediately. That usually meant something was not good and this instance was in keeping with that theory.

I quickly made my way to the troop commander's position where I was told that a LOH (light observation helicopter) had been shot down about two kilometers from our position. The pilot had reported observing an enemy bunker complex before he was shot down.

Having received my orders to launch a rescue mission, I hurried back to my platoon. In the interim the platoon had been placed on alert via radio and all the platoon vehicles were already quickly departing. My command track slowed enough to allow me to jump precariously on board. When GIs are in trouble, other GIs always respond as quickly and in every way possible. In retrospect I am reminded of the old saying "There they go, I must hasten after them for I am their leader."

The platoon sergeant was in the lead vehicle and was leading the platoon down the road as fast as the vehicles would go. Along with the urgency of the situation, he knew that most mines in the road would have a small time delay. If triggered, the mine would theoretically detonate after the vehicle had passed if we were going fast enough. Fortunately, we did not hit any mines that day.

We left the road and traveled through a large grassy area and then jungle to the last reported position of the downed helicopter. We received a radio message stating the crew of the helicopter had been safely retrieved by another helicopter in the area. While that was a relief, we still had to deal with the reported bunker complex.

About two hundred yards from the suspected bunker complex, I ordered my tracks into a line formation to provide protective fires for our hastily formed dismounted patrol.

The dismounted patrol of about fifteen men was led by me. We carefully approached the suspected enemy position. A short way in, we were confronted by a sight that would strike fear in the heart of any rational soldier. It was a line of US Army claymore mines deployed straight at us. We looked for trip wires thinking it might be a "booby trap." We found no trip wires and determined the mines were meant to be detonated on command by the defenders of the enemy complex.

We were able to crawl past the claymores without incident. We found and cleared the bunker complex and surrounding area without finding any enemy soldiers. They had obviously fled only a few minutes before our arrival. Had they chosen to fight, it would have been a very bad day for my platoon because of the claymore mines.

We secured the area of the bunkers and received orders to mount our vehicles. The troop commander had arrived with a sister platoon and we joined them to sweep the area for enemy soldiers seeking to elude us.

As we swept the area, we passed the downed helicopter. The tail and rotors were broken off and only the cabin area remained intact. The break away design had allowed the helicopter crew to escape the crash with little or no injury.

When the area was secure, we returned to the bunker complex. Analysis of the contents revealed that it had been a small field hospital replete with bandages and other basic medical supplies. Much to our surprise, we even found clothing items indicating at least some females had staffed the hospital.

That day brought reinforcement to my knowledge that GIs will give everything to support their fellow GIs. It also reminded me that even the best of plans do not ensure safety or success. All the more reason, to know my job and to plan for as many contingencies as possible.

EXCEPTIONS

Let me be very clear concerning my admiration for the American soldier. In almost every case I experienced men who although afraid, as any sane person would be, did whatever was asked of them without question and with total disregard for their own immediate well being.

Unfortunately, I was aware of a few exceptions. It might not be politically correct to call them cowards, but I am at a loss for a more appropriate descriptive term.

The first instance involved another platoon leader in a sister squadron. The platoon was ambushed on a narrow road with heavy forestation along one shoulder.

The platoon leader was, of course, expected to immediately direct return fire and defensively position his platoon. Instead, he fell to the bottom of the tank he was riding and cowered. The platoon sergeant took charge of the platoon and successfully repelled the attack. By chance, the platoon sergeant lost his life in the fight. The offending platoon leader, to my knowledge, was not court martialed. He was simply relieved of command and given a "soft" job in a rear area. At least he could not endanger others there. His only punishment, that was visible to me, was that he was effectively shunned by his fellow officers. I knew of no officer that would acknowledge his presence in any way other than in the conduct of official business.

The second instance involved one of my platoon medics. Upon receiving very heavy incoming fire on our position, he fell to the floor of his track and began reading the bible aloud. He was not a combatant, so that action in itself was not too bad. When I became aware of wounded engineers behind our line, he disregarded my order to go to their aid. That was his job! I won't go into detail, but after going to his track and counseling him, he did finally go to the wounded soldiers. To be blunt, he was more afraid of me than he was the enemy. He had good reason to feel that way. It was not long before I was able to get him out of my platoon and get a real medic and soldier.

Sometimes a leader has to recognize that certain people just do not measure up to what is expected of them. At that point the leader has to take action to ensure the well being and mission capability of his unit.

LEECHES

Although we were a mounted unit, spending the vast majority of our time on or near our armored vehicles, terrain, weather, and other considerations sometimes required us to conduct patrols on foot.

Of course we occasionally had to cross streams and swampy areas. The streams, especially during the monsoon season, tended to be very cold and swift and normally had vegetation growing right up to the water. The swampy areas were normally wide and very muddy with lots of standing rancid water.

Except for the added difficulties of securing our position and poor communication with our support troops, the wet area operations were very similar to other dismounted patrols.

As we waded through, or were required to lay prone for whatever reason, we often acquired little uninvited passengers. My first exposure worried me because I did not know what they were. They appeared to be small roundworms roughly one inch long and aggressively attached themselves to our skin by biting and not letting go. I soon learned they were leeches and were comparatively harmless other than minor skin irritation and, of course, the shock factor of seeing them attached to us.

It was my impression that leeches, at least the ones I had seen in the United States, were flat and appear to be leaves until they have dined on their victim and swelled up. Must have been a different variety in Asia. I was assured they were leeches.

The remedy to remove them was to spray them with the insect repellant we kept on our tracks. They would then fall off after a minute or so. We, of course, had to endure them until we completed the patrol mission and returned to our tracks.

Guess they were harmless, but I've never met anyone who liked the idea of having a bunch of little round blood suckers attached to the various parts of their body.

LETTERS AND FUDGE

A common element in a soldier's life is loneliness. Wars are fought in distant places far away from friends and loved ones. Of course, the holidays are normally the toughest times, loneliness is a persistent force. New friends are made and the companionship of fellow soldiers helps to pass the time and is often greatly enjoyed. That said, however, Dorothy was right when she said "There's no place like home."

We regularly received "care packages" from the Red Cross. The packages contained personal items such as soap and toothpaste and were often laden with candy. The candy did not always fare so well in the tropical conditions. The Hershey bars were almost white either from the heat or age, but, were still relished. Down deep we knew the packages meant that somebody cared enough to think of us.

In the early 1970s we did not have the luxury of computers and mobile phones. A few lucky individuals at a main base camp were occasionally permitted to make a brief call to their loved ones via the MARS station. All other contact with home was limited to mail. Sometimes the mail would appear fairly regularly and other times it could take a month or more to reach the soldier. Still, any news from home was marvelous and gave us a moment to think of those we missed so much.

The letters from my parents, grandparents, and brother were always the highlight of the day. They provided news of home and were a way of connecting long distance. It meant so much to know how much they cared for me. Letters from my girlfriend, and other friends helped me to remember and look forward to the great life waiting at home. Perhaps an exception was a letter I received from my good friend Jerry Hill. He had a good and respected career as a navy pilot, but that is another story. Jerry's letter contained a picture of him and his little boy with the deer they had just taken in hunting season. It was great to hear from Jerry, but the fact that he was having such a great time with his family made me homesick. I still chide him about the picture, but he seems to decline to feel guilty. I think the problem was mine.

My dear mother was a great lady and a great cook. She frequently sent packages from home with cookies and other goodies. On several occasions she sent chocolate fudge. Now please remember that the climate was tropical and it required as much as a month for me to receive the packages from home. I can still see her in her kitchen cutting the candy into neat squares and lovingly placing them one by one inside a metal coffee can so they would arrive unbroken. Needless to say, when they finally arrived, all the neat little pieces were melted into a large glob of chocolate syrup. Since I was a highly trained soldier it was up to me to improvise. I passed out plastic spoons to a few of my fellow troopers and we all dug into the goo. It tasted just right and was a great little piece of home. It was many years before I shared the true story with my dear mother.

It was sometimes difficult to write letters home. There was an innate feeling that I was only allowed to send positive news and should do nothing to worry those at home. I like most young men thought I was pretty slick. Years later I was privileged to read the letters sent to my parents, which they had saved in a neat little package. I was appalled at how my letters increasingly revealed the truth and how hardened I had become. While I was in Cambodia, everything was covered with red mud. It was impossible to keep anything clean including the letters and envelopes. Later in my tour my hand was injured by a piece of shrapnel rendering my writing ability useless. Knowing that silence would be worrisome, a friend was kind enough to write a letter as I dictated. The letter forced me to admit I was unable to write but stressed that the injury was minor and that things were generally all right. Does anyone succeed in fooling their mother?

Soldiers are still people. We all need to know that others care and that there is always hope for a better life. The letters and packages from home were a fragile thread that did wondrous things in helping us keep some semblance of sanity. After all, we needed to know that no matter what our personal reasons for being where we were, the important things in life were safe and there waiting for us.

BOREDOM

The battlefield is a strange place to be. It is often filled with emotions ranging from sheer terror to times when one seems to have absolutely nothing to do except to wonder why in the world you are sitting where you are.

Although most days and nights were busy with patrols or maintenance duties, there were times when it seems the old army adage of "hurry up and wait" was stretched to the extreme.

The slow times were usually used to get a little much needed rest, although we still had to maintain guard duty and be ever vigilant. After letter writing, bathing as best we could, and other menial tasks, we would spend the time napping, playing cards, talking, or just staring at the countryside and often dreaming of home.

As a leader, it was challenging to balance "down time" with activity. My troopers, like all young men, just seemed to be happier when they were gainfully occupied.

Boredom is just one more of the myriad things that have to be dealt with in a combat zone.

BETEL NUT

It was a warm and sunny day in the dry season. There had been very little action for several days, and it was almost a relief to conduct yet another search-and-destroy mission.

We were moving along the edge of a large grassy field and were in the very edge of a rubber plantation. It was an easy recon mission considering the generally open terrain did not seem to afford many good hiding places for the enemy.

We soon approached a small group of huts, two or three at the most. One hut was larger than most and was not the kind we were used to seeing. It did have the normal grass roof and fairly open walls with open windows. It was built on stilts, three or four feet high and had a wooden plank floor. It even had wide wooden steps leading up to the entrance. One wondered if it might house administration for some level of local government since it was so different from a typical home in the area. It was nestled in a sparse grove of trees and located on the main dirt road.

I deployed the platoon into a defensive perimeter around the huts and ordered a dismounted search of the area. Because there were no inhabitants in view, we were especially vigilant for booby traps. Of course, the troop commander was advised by radio of the actions we were taking.

One of the dismounted troopers soon summoned me to the largest hut saying there was something unusual he felt I needed to see.

It did not take long for me to recognize what he had seen that was concerning to the trooper. The entire wooden floor and the steps all appeared to be heavily soaked with blood.

I immediately cautioned the entire platoon to be on high alert. It seemed that anything unusual that we did not understand probably meant trouble.

Could it have been the sight of the slaughter of locals who were not loyal to the Viet Cong? Could there have been a serious battle there? Could it be a Viet Cong field Hospital evacuated when the enemy saw us approaching? In any of the possible scenarios, it was highly probable that a significant enemy force was nearby.

I immediately notified the troop commander and requested preplanned artillery fires around our position. The troop commander agreed the situation was potentially serious and immediately ordered one of my sister armored cavalry platoons to reinforce us. The troop commander joined the other platoon in route to our position.

The troop commander had, of course, also advised the squadron commander of the situation. In just a few minutes a couple of Huey helicopters equipped with rocket launchers and machine guns were circling the area above us. They were soon joined by the squadron commander, a Lieutenant Colonel, who used his helicopter to view the battlefield in large scale operations and provide direction to us as he coordinated whatever additional combat support that might be necessary. It was not unusual to see these reactions in a heavy firefight, but no shots had yet been fired. It was comforting to know we had immediate support if things did turn out to be nasty.

As my platoon sergeant and I discussed the situation, we determined the highest probability was that we were on the site of an evacuated field hospital. Although I really did not trust my Chu Hoi, a former North Vietnamese soldier assigned as my interpreter, I ordered him to look at the scene and give us his thoughts. He appeared to be puzzled for a few minutes and then began to laugh.

I, of course, asked him what he found to be so amusing. He did apologize for his laughter and gave the following explanation.

The local people did not have the advantage of dentist and good oral hygiene as we know it. As a result, the majority of them had rotten teeth and infected gums a large part of their lives. They had learned through the centuries that relief could be obtained by chewing a local nut called the Betel Nut. Its anesthetic qualities relieved the pain and was used on a daily basis. Much like old men in the good old USA would chew tobacco and spit the juice wherever they were, the Betel Nut juice was spit anywhere and everywhere. Please note that babies were diaperless in their culture, so spitting the juice on the floor was not seen as a problem to the locals.

The Betel Nut produced a deep red juice that very closely resembled dried blood on the wooden planks. Aha! We had the answer and it was an answer we liked. There would be no major battle at that position. We determined that a few locals or at the most a few enemy soldiers had inhabited the huts and were long gone.

I was a little worried since my recon had resulted in such a large military reaction. Nobody I know likes to look foolish in the eyes of their commanding officers. My worries were without basis. Both the troop commander and the squadron commander praised our platoon for our vigilance, and freely admitted that they too had learned something new.

As always, so much to learn and so little time to do it considering the consequences of bad decisions through ignorance of the situation.

C RATION WEAPON

Even with the best laid plans and lots of experience, things don't always go the way we want them to go.

It was a sunny afternoon and we were performing a mounted patrol in a reasonably dense jungle area. It was generally quiet and our point vehicle was able to crush the lower vegetation enough to create a narrow trail.

The purpose of the patrol was not out of the ordinary. We hoped to find enemy bunker complexes, engage the enemy, or at least keep the enemy off balance by showing there was no safe haven for them in the area.

I had been ordered to utilize a slightly different tactic on this day. The platoon was to make sweeping circles in the area coming back on the original trails we had made and then to follow those trails. I did not see the usefulness in this approach since it seemed unlikely to me that the enemy would move in behind us on the trails we had forged. Even so, we certainly would not catch them by surprise if they did so. There is something about ten armored vehicles crashing through the jungle that tends to make a lot of noise. Mounted stealth was not one of our primary advantages.

We had followed the circling procedure for several hours when our lead vehicle spotted something in the trail. Woody, my track commander was very experienced and volunteered to investigate.

We, of course, moved to a defensive posture known as a herringbone and Woody dismounted. He soon reported that it was a C ration box.

Woody carefully examined the box and carefully began to open it. He was immediately overcome by a noxious substance. We called for a medevac flight to take him to the squadron aid station for evaluation. Fortunately, he was not seriously hurt and soon returned to rejoin the platoon. The box had contained tear gas rigged to be dispersed on whoever opened the box. The enemy was sly and we were thankful it was not an explosive charge.

The enemy had obviously figured out our tactic of circling back and left us a message. We did not use that tactic again.

CHU HOI

The close proximity to the Vietnamese people was always problematic. Since for the most part, we were fighting an insurgency, it was often difficult to tell which Vietnamese civilians were our allies as opposed to those who were our enemy. It would have been nice if everyone had worn a sign accurately identifying them as friend or foe. That, of course, was not the case.

Since few, if any of our troopers spoke the Vietnamese language, we were often in need of an interpreter. This was necessary for communication both with the civilian population and the South Vietnamese Military personnel with whom we interacted.

The US Army solution was to provide us with a Chu Hoi. The Chu Hoi assigned to us was ostensibly a former North Vietnamese soldier who understood the enemy's tactics and could serve as an interpreter as needed. He was a part of our platoon and was always at hand for advice or to fulfill interpretation needs.

His story was that he and his brother had many years before been conscripted into the North Vietnamese Army against their wishes. Their family was threatened with execution if the brothers did not fight for the North Vietnamese Army. According to our Chu Hoi, his brother eventually deserted and the North Vietnamese made good on the threat to murder their family. After that occurred, there was nothing to keep our Chu Hoi from deserting too.

Even though the story was certainly plausible to me, I always kept a close eye on the Chu Hoi and seriously questioned any advice he rendered. Even in his role as an interpreter, I was very wary. After all, I did not know what was really being related to him by the Vietnamese speaker. The story would have simply been too easy to fabricate for the purpose of infiltrating our unit or simply to get a good paying job. He never seemed to have the fire in his soul or hatred I would have expected him to harbor against the North Vietnamese.

One instance that made me wary, occurred near a South Vietnamese village we were operating around. The terrain was fairly open and flat allowing for visibility of at least a kilometer or more. We woke one morning to see the dirt road leading from the village had gained a crude barrier during the night. The Chu Hoi advised the sign on the barrier warned villagers that the Viet Cong had mined the road. This was apparently a propaganda effort to show the villagers that the Viet Cong was still in control of the area in spite of our presence.

Nothing was suspicious except that the Chu Hoi was adamant that the road was not mined and was safe for us to use as usual. He asserted that the warning sign and barricade were just placed to slow us down and occupy our time.

As usual, I chose to be cautious. As our troopers swept the road for mines, we found and destroyed two antitank mines. Had we taken the Chu Hoi's advice, we would undoubtedly have sustained at least some equipment damage and probably casualties.

Was the Chu Hoi lying to lead us into a trap, or was he simply wrong in his analysis of the situation? I will never know. If it seems too good to be true, it probably is.

FO (FORWARD OBSERVER),
LEAVE ME ALONE

Artillery support was, of course, a very important part of our fighting capability. It gave us the advantage of relatively long range support when we were far from other friendly forces. It had the capability of providing devastating firepower beyond our line of sight in the forested areas. It provided the ability to intercept the enemy on avenues of approach and retreat. On at least one occasion, when we were about to be over run, airburst danger close to our position successfully repelled the enemy. The use of artillery support was limited generally only by our imagination in ways to deploy its awesome firepower. Yes, in most cases were thankful for the support of our artillery, usually provided by our squadrons 155 gun battery.

As in all things there were exceptions. One such time found us on a search-and-destroy mission far from our Troop Headquarters and sister platoons.

We had experienced another long hot day and had just established our platoon defensive perimeter for the night. It was approximately five o'clock in the evening and we were looking forward to a little food and what rest we could manage. We were in a fairly clear area with good open fields of fire and just happened to be on a dirt trail leading to the village not far down into a valley below.

I knew exactly where we were located and had reported my exact position to our Troop Headquarters. The landmarks were clear and there could be no doubt as to the accuracy of our location.

Admittedly, in dense terrain it would have been difficult to give an exact location.

A call came on the radio from our artillery battery located at Troop Headquarters. It was common for them to register their guns by firing a spotter round. The procedure should have been simple. They would fire an airburst somewhere in my vicinity and I would tell them exactly where the round had exploded. They would then have their needed reference points to provide supporting fires as needed.

They fired their first spotter round and asked me for the exact location of where it had exploded. This presented a problem in that even with our clear lines of sight we did not hear or see the round explode. Since I was sure of my location, I knew they either did not have my location recorded accurately or they had a significant flaw in their firing data.

After about five or six hours of repeated spotter rounds having been fired without a successful sighting, my nerves were getting frayed. Obviously I wanted the needed artillery support, but this was getting ridiculous and I was exhausted.

I'm sure the artillery folks were getting tired of the process too. Someone, who did not identify himself, came on the radio and insisted that I had given a bad location for my unit and was basically a blankety-blank idiot.

Before I could respond, our troop forward observer, who worked for the artillery battery commander, came on the radio and urged them to forget the exercise and leave me alone. That was gutsy on his part, but he had worked with my unit enough to know we knew what we were doing.

The next voice on the radio was music to my ears. It was the squadron commander. He was addressing the artillery commander and was very succinct. He said that he had complete faith that our platoon was located exactly where I said we were, that the resupply helicopters had no trouble finding me in that exact position, that the artillery folks were directed to stop harassing me, and that the artillery folks would figure out what their problem was and advise him at the squadron briefing the following day.

I was wise enough to just be thankful and not offer any further comment.

Please do not interpret this as a slam on the artillery folks. They are generally great and are our brothers in arms. Some days at the office in the jungle just aren't exactly as you would like them to be.

SHORT-TIME GIRLS

I believe every war brings unexpected surprises for the soldiers in dealing with the indigenous people in the war zone. I am sure like everywhere in the world, most of the local people are concerned with survival and living within the bounds of their culture. Many are displaced, or at least greatly inconvenienced and adapt as best they can.

In Vietnam we seemed to be besieged by those we called "short time girls." They were mostly young women who traveled on mopeds (small motorcycles) and seemed to be everywhere except the deepest jungle areas.

Many carried small coolers on their mopeds and at least pretended to be selling cold coca colas. In reality, many of them were prostitutes, drug suppliers, and quite frankly spies for the Viet Cong.

Two situations made it very difficult and mostly impossible to keep them away from our troops.

First, our troopers were young men far from home and easily attracted to anyone that they felt could provide them with female companionship. The local girls were generally not very attractive by our standards at home, but they were available.

Secondly, a large part of our efforts were geared to gaining the support of the local population. Any drastic measures to keep the local girls at bay would have had repercussions.

Their existence was not always a disadvantage. I do not recall ever having receiving incoming fire when the short-time girls were in the area. Additionally, if they were not in an area where we expected them to be, it was a pretty good sign that we had better be on high alert.

One of the most interesting experiences with the short-time girls occurred when I was acting troop commander.

The squadron commander came to our location and spoke with me privately. He ordered me to move to a new location known only to him and me. He ordered the move to commence in less than one hour. The new location was about eight kilometers away and in the general vicinity of a huge grassy plain.

We commenced our movement of the entire troop, over forty armored vehicles and several hundred troopers. I would relay instructions to the lead platoon every few hundred meters since I was prohibited from telling anyone what our final destination was to be.

After about one and one-half hours, I could see the general area of our new site. I looked at my terrain map and the lay of the terrain to decide exactly where I should establish the new NDP. Please remember that the Squadron Commander had only given me a general area within which to locate, and even I didn't know the exact final location until we were almost there.

Yes, you guessed it! In the middle of the huge plain and far from the nearest road, several short-time girls were waiting for us. Perhaps their ability to select the most likely tactical location in the general area could be explained. How they knew what area we were headed to, I will never know. Their intelligence system was not to be under-estimated.

SLOPPY JOES

Food, or chow as we affectionately called it, is very important to the soldier for many reasons. Of course, we expended a lot of energy and need the calories and nutrition. Although, we could not gather for our meals in the field, "breaking bread" almost always has a good social effect. A hot meal was one of the few comforts we could experience even if "Mom" wasn't there to prepare it for us.

When we were fortunate enough to be in a main base, we were able to eat in the unit mess hall. The food was almost always, hot, tasty, nourishing, and served in enormous quantities. I never saw anyone leave the mess hall complaining that they were still hungry.

Getting food in the field was not always so easy. We were well supported and had our MREs, which were much tastier than the old C-rations. Occasionally we had LRP meals. They came in a larger bag and were meant to feed eight to ten soldiers. Just add hot water. Since we did not exactly have running hot water, we would either heat the water by holding it over a small piece of burning C-4 explosive or by placing the water container on the vehicle exhaust. The meal was reasonably tasty and came in several varieties. Chili-con-carne was my favorite.

Not always, but on many days, the evening supply helicopter would bring us several mermite containers of hot food along with our ammunition etc. The mermite containers were essentially large thermos containers specifically made for holding and serving prepared meals. The food would still be hot and tasty just as it was when it was shipped from the mess hall in the rear area. A typical meal requiring three or four mermite containers might consists of meat-loaf, green beans, carrots, mashed potatoes and gravy. Enough was provided to feed the platoon.

One evening meal proved to be rather disappointing. We had been on patrol for some time and had not enjoyed a hot meal in several days.

The supply helicopter arrived shortly before dusk. To our glee, three mermite cans were unloaded for us. We were ready for a good hot meal.

As things sometimes go, our joy was short lived. Upon opening the mermite cans, we discovered they all contained the meat for sloppy joe sandwiches. There was no bread, chips, or anything else. It was obviously an error in the supply system.

I notified troop headquarters and was advised that a sister platoon had received enough sandwich bread for the entire troop and another platoon had received all the cake meant for the troop.

My troopers were hungry, so I instructed them to open one mermite can and dive in with their canteen cups. It wasn't very tasty, but at least it was food. A few hours after dark the supply helicopter arrived at our location again. Delivering supplies at night was dangerous work for the helicopter crew, but they always tried to help us any way they could. We quickly loaded the extra mermite cans as the crew threw numerous loaves of bread at us. We never saw the cake, but at least we got to eat and I believe the sister platoons probably finally got their meat.

One learns to be happy for the little things.

ANTS

It was just another routine search-and-destroy mission. The weather was clear and warm in the early afternoon. The ground was soft in a few places because of recent rain.

The mission required the platoon to go a few kilometers on a jungle trail. The trail reached a point where fairly dense jungle was on our right side and the left side was a clearing extending for about 100 yards wide. The clearing was a marshy area that obviously would not support the traffic of our armored vehicles. There were no villages nearby, which made our mission a little easier. There was no apparent reason for civilians to be in the area. Any one seen was presumed to be the enemy.

Without warning, we received RPG (rocket propelled grenade) and AK 47 rifle fire from our right flank. The immediate action was to form a Herringbone formation and return fire. The Herringbone formation meant that each vehicle turned to the right or left alternatively to ensure three hundred and sixty degree observation and fields of fire. The formation also ensured that if we were overrun by the enemy, the next vehicle could spray the adjacent vehicles with machine-gun fire to clear them of attacking enemy soldiers.

As was always the case, the enemy was well hidden. It was a difficult process to evaluate the threat, report to the troop commander, and return the most effective fire.

I had been in country long enough to know that the best defense was to attack with effective fire and maneuver. The platoon immediately fired all weapons including machine guns, M79 grenade launchers, and fléchette rounds from the tanks. As I was firing my machine gun, I used the radio to gather information from my track commanders since I could not see the whole battlefield because of the dense jungle. I requested artillery fire to be preplanned to block the enemy's escape. After all, our mission was to find and kill the enemy.

The incoming fire was very heavy indicating a fairly sizeable enemy force. We remained in our positions while I assessed the situation. It was clear that at least some of the enemy soldiers were very close to us. I directed all the track commanders to turn their vehicles toward the enemy to ensure the most effective fire. Since the area then behind us was a clearing with good visibility, it was unlikely that we would be attacked from that direction. As a precaution, I reminded the track commanders to ensure at least one crew member was watching the area behind their vehicle.

As the intensity of incoming fire increased, so did my concern. Usually, our heavy firepower was sufficient to cause the enemy to stay down, thus reducing their ability to aim accurately or deliver a significant volume of fire.

On my left front, I noticed what I thought could have been a camouflaged opening to a tunnel or one man spider hole. In an effort to eliminate the possible threat, I threw a hand grenade at the opening and told my crew to get down. I don't know if the hole was occupied or not, but that potential threat was eliminated.

After a very short time, the troop commander ordered me to attack the enemy. He had ordered a sister platoon to take a position that would intercept the enemy's flank as we drove them back. Of course, we would also shell the suspected enemy positions using the preplanned artillery targets I had requested earlier in the fight.

The platoon moved forward in a line formation. We did not get far. Another lesson was about to be learned. It seems there is a type of ant in that area of the world that builds its nest high in the jungle trees. The nest is simply a large leaf about six to eight inches long that the ants fold into a pocket and cement together with saliva. The leaves are still attached to the trees and are basically suspended in the open.

We knew the enemy was clever. As we moved forward, the trees were disturbed by our vehicles causing the ants to fall directly on us by the thousands. Now one might assume this would be a nuisance but not enough to degrade our combat capability. When the ants fell on us, there was nothing we could do. Their stings were so powerful we were unable to do anything other than try to get the ants off of us. We were probably quite a sight to see, but I saw no humor in the situation. The enemy, I will always believe, had chosen their ambush site to take advantage of the ants. It worked, although it only took a few minutes to get the ants under control using the insecticide spray we all carried, it was enough time for the enemy to withdraw from the area without being seen or accurately fired upon. Who would have thought a few nests of ants could neutralize the massive firepower of an Armored Cavalry Platoon?

When we could, we moved forward, but received no further incoming fire, nor did we find any enemy dead or wounded. Combat is deceiving. It seemed that the battle lasted for hours, but, it lasted ten minutes at the most. One heck of a way to break the boredom.

Yes, we lost that battle in my mind. It was the closest our platoon came to failing to accomplish the mission. Fortunately, my commanders did not agree. They felt the mission was a success in that we had a least verified a sizeable enemy unit was in the area and had done so without taking casualties.

AVIATORS

Our primary interaction with aviators was in the form of helicopter pilots who performed a variety of missions crucial to our survival. Yes, we did have support from the US Air Force, but this was normally at arm's length. In other words, we seldom had direct interaction with the Air Force.

I will attempt to describe some of the aviation missions and what they meant to the troops on the ground. First, let me make it very clear that almost without fail, the helicopter pilots performed their missions no matter what the risk to them personally. I believe they truly understood that their efforts were crucial to mission accomplishment and their actions contributed significantly to the survival of the troops on the ground.

The army aviators seemed to be a fairly wild bunch. They displayed a tremendous amount of esprit de corps and strove hard to enjoy life to the best of their ability. Let us just say that when they could, they knew how to party.

We knew we could count on them, and sometimes they were genuinely kind. One such occasion was on Christmas Eve. The resupply chopper sat down at my location, and the pilot motioned for me to come to his side window. The dust was great from his whirling rotors and the noise was deafening. When I approached him, he smiled widely and handed me a bottle of Scotch Whiskey. I knew he was wishing me a merry Christmas and showing that he genuinely cared for us as we struggled in the world of ground-based troops. I did not know him and probably never saw him again. Once again, the power of the bond between GIs was shown to me.

One of the most impressive missions to me was that of the LOH (light observation helicopter) scouts. They were small two-seater aircraft, normally manned only by the pilot, and were assigned directly to our squadron. Their primary mission was to observe in front of our mounted patrols as we advanced on search-and-destroy missions. They could have done a fairly good job of this by flying high in safety. That was not the way they worked. They would go back and forth along our projected path looking for bunkers, signs of movement, etc. They would typically fly about ten meters above the terrain. They seemed sometimes to think they were invincible. Their real job was to alert us of any obstacles or danger they saw and then get out of our way. After all, we had the armored vehicles and immense firepower. Instead, on more than one occasion, I saw them hover just four or five feet above the ground, using their prop wash to blow the vegetation aside so they could see better. On one occasion, I even saw the pilot lean out and roll a grenade into a bunker he had spotted. Although we appreciated their actions, which undoubtedly saved lives, I always wished they would have just done their job by reporting what they saw and letting us handle it. They were GIs too, and we did not want to see them hurt. Additionally, they would have been of no further use to us if they were shot down.

As mentioned elsewhere, the supply missions of the helicopter pilots were crucial. In our field locations, we would receive ammunition, food, mail, and sometimes even a coveted block of ice via the Huey helicopters. The squadron NDP often was serviced by the larger Chinook helicopters capable of transporting more troops and heavier loads such as fuel and water bladders. The supply missions were always hazardous because the enemy knew where we were located and the helicopters made attractive targets. The resupply missions also provided a means of transportation for individuals needing to go to the main base camp or other areas. And of course, if we had wounded, the resupply helicopters would evacuate them if possible.

The Medevac missions were primarily conducted by Hueys designated as air ambulances. They had a large Red Cross painted on each side to show them as noncombatants under the rules of the Geneva Convention. In reality, the Red Cross made an attractive target for the enemy. The medevac crew never failed us. No matter what the weather, day or night, and the amount of incoming fire, they were always there to get our wounded out of the field and to the field hospital. When the medevac would land, we would increase our rate of outgoing fires as much as possible in an effort to decrease the enemy rate of fire and accuracy. Our troops would hurriedly load the wounded on the medivac in any manner they could. Our troops would then return to the fight as we lessened our fires along the route the helicopter would travel as it left our area. Obviously, we did not want to shoot down our own medevac helicopters.

The US Army gunships consisted of two types. Of course, all the Hueys were armed with M60 machine guns. These often proved helpful, but the real firepower was in the Cobra helicopters. They were heavily armed with rockets and miniguns. When enemy soldiers were identified, they would follow the nap of the earth, enabling them to attack without warning. Because they flew so close to the ground, they could provide devastating fires for very close support without fear of hitting our positions by mistake. Their ability to fire and observe from above made it very difficult for the enemy to seek effective cover or concealment.

The US Air Force played a significant role on several occasions. Although they were able to provide heavier firepower than our army helicopters, their accuracy was far less than the helicopters, rendering them less desirable for close support. We seemed to have an aversion to the thought of being accidentally bombed or strafed by our friendly aircraft.

On two occasions, we were supported by fighter bombers. When we were told that the fighter bombers were coming, we would pull back at least three hundred meters from the area to be bombed. A small air force spotter aircraft would then fire marker rounds to identify the area for the air strike. As the fighter bombers swooped in, we were presented with quite a show of firepower. The napalm bombs seemed to engulf the entire area. I would not have wanted to be on the receiving end of their miniguns and rockets. Needless to say, the enemy no longer fired upon us. I was puzzled; however, we knew the enemy had been there because we had been fighting them. But after the airstrikes, we could not find a trace of the enemy when we searched the area. Had the napalm totally consumed them, or had they somehow been able to move before the airstrike? I guess I will never know.

Sometimes it took a while for the fighter bombers to arrive. One morning we had been receiving rocket fire in our Squadron NDP. The air force spotter plane was able to identify the enemy firing position. When he called for attack aircraft, he was told it would be about thirty minutes before they arrived. I suppose he knew, as we did, that the enemy would have been long gone before the attack aircraft arrived. He decided to hit the position with his marker rounds and I believe a limited number of rockets. Problem solved. No more incoming fire from that position. We knew what he was doing because our forward observer was in radio contact with him.

Another area of support provided by the US Air Force was in the form of I believe C-130 aircraft affectionately known to us as "Snoopy" and "Puff the Magic Dragon." They were called upon by our higher headquarters to eliminate suspected areas of enemy concentration not easily accessible or in close proximity to us. Although I only saw them used twice, they were apparently quite effective. The strikes occurred at night obscuring our view of the aircraft and the strike zone. What we did see was what appeared to be a thin red thread originating high in the sky and terminating on the ground beyond our range of vision. The red thread we saw was actually the tracer rounds from the high rate of fire miniguns on the aircraft. We were told that they covered an area approximately the size of a football field and ensured at least one round struck every square foot of the area. We were never sent to evaluate the results, I am sure some other unit did, but I was relieved to know that was one less potential threat with which we would have to contend. Besides, the tracer show was awesome to behold.

The air force also provided night illumination a few times. Their parachute flares would seemingly turn the night into day and would be provided as long as our commanders felt we needed them. Personally I preferred the darkness in most instances. If we could see the enemy, they could see us. There were times, of course, when we had to retrieve vehicles, etc., and the flares made the task much easier, quicker, and generally safer. Anyway, their use was at the discretion of my commanders.

All things considered, our air support played a number of vital roles. I soon became keenly aware that airpower alone could not win wars and seldom even individual battles. The dirty work still had to be done by troops on the ground.

ACCIDENTAL FIRE

Accidental fire can and does occur in many ways. It can be the result of mishandling weapons, miscalculations, equipment malfunctions, or so called "friendly fire."

I had the misfortune to witness the results of all of the above. Heavy equipment and a multitude of weapons always constitute a hazardous environment. Add the stress and confusion of combat to these hazards, and the potential risks become very high.

The first casualty of which I was aware, occurred not in my presence but very nearby. Some troopers were firing pistols into the jungle away from the squadron NDP. I do not know whether they were firing for practice or checking their weapons. There was a sudden commotion and I soon discovered that one of the troopers had mishandled his pistol resulting in a gunshot wound to the abdomen of the trooper beside him. The trooper was soon placed on a medevac and unfortunately as we all anticipated died a few weeks later. We were not medical personnel, but we all knew that wounds to the abdomen would probably result in a fatal infection.

One afternoon, as I was walking just inside the outer perimeter of the troop NDP in a sister platoon's area, I heard a commotion. I looked at the rear of a nearby track and saw two troopers "horsing-around." One trooper yelled something similar to "give me my rifle" as he grabbed the barrel of an M-16 rifle held by another trooper. I tried to yell at them to stop, but it was too late. The rifle discharged killing the trooper. Of course, we tried to help him, but it was just not possible. Two lives ruined. The trooper who lost his life and the other trooper whom I am sure has never forgotten the memory of accidentally killing his friend and fellow trooper. Weapons are serious business. I am sure that is why I treat weapons as necessary tools to be respected and properly utilized. Weapons are not toys. They are designed to kill and do so without regard for anyone.

I had been a platoon leader for only a few days. Our platoon was located at the troop NDP along with one of our sister platoons. As I was walking toward the troop command track I heard a loud commotion. It was a sister platoon's platoon sergeant loudly berating a soldier for not having cleaned his machine gun as he had apparently been told to do several times. The soldier was clearly very angry as he returned to his track. A few moments later, I heard the unmistakable sound of a burst of M60 machine gun fire. The soldier had apparently started to dismantle the weapon for cleaning without unloading the weapon. The accidental discharge, unfortunately seriously wounded a trooper on the adjacent track. Once again, stupidity had resulted in serious injury to a trooper. I never saw the offending trooper after that morning. I always assumed that he had been sent to the rear area to remove him from the other troopers in his platoon. I do not know if or how he was punished. I have always hoped that he was court martialed.

On a particular sunny and dry day in S. Vietnam, our platoon search-and-destroy mission was interrupted by a change of mission. A sister platoon was in a heavy engagement and we were ordered to assist them. As we neared the objective, a grove of trees perhaps seventy-five yards wide and about three hundred yards long, the land was free of trees but was very hilly. The objective obviously contained enemy troops who were delivering a heavy volume of small arms fire. I placed my platoon in a line formation and moved in the direction the troop commander indicated. All three of the troop's platoons were moving toward the objective. Unfortunately, because of the hilly terrain, we did not have visual contact with our sister platoons. All three platoons were laying down a heavy base of fire as we approached the objective. After a few minutes, urgent orders to cease fire and hold our positions were heard on the troop radio net. It seems that the movements of our platoons without visual contact had resulted in some troopers actually receiving fire from sister platoons. We were fortunate that no troopers were wounded. The troop commander ordered us all to back off about three hundred yards from the objective and ensure that no enemy soldiers could escape the tree line. He then called in jet fighters to attack the objective with napalm. The attack appeared to be successful, but we were able to find no sign of the enemy soldiers when we cleared the area. Well, at least we had not suffered any losses because of friendly fire in the confusion of the battle.

Of course some friendly fire is the result of equipment malfunction. Occasionally a mortar round or artillery round will miss the target because of equipment failure. One such instance occurred while we were in Cambodia. A young trooper had moved just forward of our position to answer the call of Mother Nature. As was common practice, a fellow trooper overwatched him from his M60 machine-gun position for his safety. As the trooper began his business he was hit in the buttocks by shrapnel from a mortar round. It took only a few moments to realize the mortar round was not incoming fire, but instead, was a short round fired by our own mortar crew just a few hundred feet behind our tracks. The round had only traveled a few hundred feet. Of course, the mortar round was an inanimate object and did not differentiate between enemy and friendly troops. The wounded trooper was attended by our medic and soon medevaced to a field hospital. Fortunately, the troopers wounds were not life threatening. I think he was more angry than hurt. He had completed his tour of duty and was scheduled to return to the United States the next day. His wounds meant his departure home would be delayed while he was treated in the field hospital. He was not a happy trooper.

CHU HOI PAMPHLETS

I had been in South Vietnam for several months and thought I could no longer be surprised by the unexpected.

We were once again on a search-and-destroy mission and had just arrived at the edge of a dirt road in what appeared to be a good place to establish our platoon NDP.

We circled our vehicles and began preparations for the night. We carefully checked the area for bobby traps and began setting out command detonated claymore mines in front of our vehicles. Someone noticed the Chu Hoi Pamphlets and called me to their location.

A Chu Hoi Pamphlet was a single sheet of paper with a message to the Viet Cong urging them to give up the fight. Loosely translated, "Chu Hoi" means I surrender. The pamphlets were part of psychological warfare operations and had probably been dropped in mass from a low flying aircraft.

The thing that made these particular pamphlets a matter of concern was the way they were displayed. Each of the three was neatly folded and placed in a small pile of human excrement, which was still fresh. The piles were in a row and about three feet apart.

Decision time. Were they marking a booby trap? Were they left there just to mess with our minds? Had the enemy carefully measured them as the center of a kill zone for their rockets and mortars?

We quickly examined the area for booby traps and found none.

When one does not have the answer, it is best to err on the side of safety. We quickly moved our NDP a few hundred meters and reported the incident. It turned out to be a quiet night. I guess they really were messing with us or if they had marked the area for rocket and mortar fire, our move put them at a disadvantage.

Lessons learned are to always be observant, expect the unexpected, and take action.

THE BRIDGE

We had been in South Vietnam for a while. Our NDP was located in an old South Vietnamese Army position overlooking the Mekong River.

The position had seen a lot of traffic over time and was void of vegetation. The berms basically formed a barrier to any proper drainage of water resulting in knee deep water and mud that were almost impossible to traverse on foot. It rained a lot so there was little relief from the stagnant water and general soggy condition. The smell was awful and we were blessed with the presence of plenty of rats.

We were generally happy to go on a search-and-destroy mission just to get away from the NDP.

Our operations were generally concentrated on the area away from the river. Aside from some open areas on the high ground and a few swampy clearings, the area was primarily a heavily forested jungle and was not really the most advantageous for operating our tracked vehicles. That, of course, meant lots of ground patrols with little support from our tracked vehicles.

We did have one serious obstacle to overcome. Because we had to move in one direction to get from the NDP to our area of operations, the volume of traffic was high and very much restricted in area. A few hundred meters from the NDP we were forced to use a narrow crossing on a small but fast flowing stream. The crossing quickly became a quagmire that we could cross slowly and with great effort. It was not reliable and certainly did not allow for rapid reinforcement should we become heavily engaged on our search-and-destroy missions.

The troop commander ordered us to build a bridge on the crossing. The majority of all three combat platoons, except for security details, participated in the effort.

I am positive that a good engineer would have seen a great deal of humor in our efforts. We did not have the luxury of correct materials, therefore, we did what any good troopers would do. We improvised.

We found some pieces of old metal culvert, about four to six feet in diameter, in the area of the NDP. It would have been nice to at least have some heavy machinery, rock, and bracing materials. The only other materials we had were sandbags.

Using sheer manpower, we all got knee deep in mud to which we were already accustomed, and laid a base of sandbags for the culvert pieces. We then placed the culvert pieces on the sandbags and secured them as best we could with a large number of sandbags.

After three or four hours of hard work, our masterpiece was complete. The bridge was only wide enough for one vehicle, but it looked like it might work. We all celebrated and took a lot of pictures of ourselves and the bridge.

It was now time to test our engineering skills. Needless to say we did not want to start by moving a 60 ton M60 main battle tank across the bridge. We did choose an ACAV as the test vehicle.

As the ACAV moved slowly onto the bridge, we were all disappointed. Everything was mashed into a flat sheet at the bottom of the creek. It did, however, keep the ACAV from miring down in the mud. It may not have looked good, but the bridge was a success. We were able to move ACAVS and tanks across it without being significantly slowed.

The bridge served us well for several days while we completed our missions. We did not have to call for reinforcements, but the knowledge that we could was comforting. It could easily have made the difference in failure or accomplishment of the mission.

A trooper must always be prepared to do whatever becomes necessary. Call it Yankee Engineering, or whatever you want, our troopers always found a way.

THE MONEY SAVER

As indicated before, the platoon was a mixture of young men with diverse backgrounds.

One young man who stood out was a machine gunner from a northern state, Michigan I believe. He was a sturdy, but not large, blonde, and probably was of Nordic descent.

One afternoon, I had the pleasure of talking with him at length. I wanted to understand what I could about my troopers. He was quiet and unassuming while being absolutely dependable.

He related the following background. He was raised in a large family in a wilderness area. His family was primarily self sufficient and he was probably the first homeschooled person I ever met. He could not attend regular school because between the first snow and the spring thaw, his family had no way to travel. They had to be fully prepared and survive the winter on their own.

When I asked him what he wanted to do after military service, he indicated he wanted to return home and live in the wilderness as he had been raised, with one exception.

He had then been in country for about ten months. He related that in that time he had only spent three dollars and a few cents. All the remainder of his pay was being placed in savings.

His dream upon returning to the "Great Post Exchange," otherwise known as the USA, was to purchase a snowmobile for his family's use. He wanted them to have freedom and access to the outside world in the winter months.

I always hoped his family realized what a fine son he was. I bet they knew it.

THE SMALL TREE

Another beautiful sunny day in the Republic of South Vietnam.

It was hot and the platoon was conducting yet another search-and-destroy mission.

The terrain was slightly hilly and was partly forested and partly open fields of grass. It was the dry season and dust was our constant companion.

The day had been fairly uneventful, which was a good thing. As we maneuvered along the edge of a wooded area, we noticed a small tree, four to six feet in height had been partially felled by an axe or a knife. The tree was bent over parallel to the ground and was still connected at its base. The foliage was still fairly green indicating it had not been long since someone had been there.

I immediately deployed the platoon in a defensive position. I had no idea of the significance of the tree. Could it indicate the presence of explosive traps, the center of fields of fire from a hidden force, a mere trail marker, or nothing of significance at all?

Because of the possibility of explosive devices I did not want a lot of boots on the ground. The threat of a hidden ambush force in the woods also required maximum vigilance and firepower on the tracks.

I elected to have one of my tank commanders and myself investigate.

The tank commander was a well educated and mild mannered Staff Sergeant. He had earned his stripes through a special NCO academy, otherwise known as "shake and bake." I found him to be reliable and effective but lacking in experience.

We carefully approached the tree looking for trip wires or anything out of the ordinary. The Sergeant was walking about eight to ten feet behind me.

After walking about thirty feet, I was knocked to the ground by the force of an explosion. My first thoughts were that we were under attack by a hidden ground force. The platoon immediately laid down defensive fires with all available weapons.

As I checked myself for wounds, fortunately I had none, I overheard someone yell the LT (lieutenant) finally got it. As always in a combat situation, the confusion was immense.

I soon realized the Sergeant behind me had been wounded by the blast. I yelled for the medic and tried to analyze the situation. It became apparent that we were not under attack, but had triggered a hidden explosive device. I ordered cease fire and yelled to the Platoon Sergeant to call for a medevac helicopter.

In talking with the medic, it appeared the Sergeant's wounds were severe but probably not life threatening if he received prompt medical help. His legs had a large number of shrapnel wounds, but it appeared his armored vest had absorbed most of the shrapnel that would surely have caused fatal wounds. The vest was shredded, but it had done the job for which it was designed.

It was only a few minutes before we had the area secured and the medevac helicopter arrived to evacuate our wounded Sergeant.

It was time to search for further booby traps and to determine what had happened. No additional explosive devices were found. We soon realize the downed tree had been a marker indicating the location of the booby trap. Whether it was meant as a marker for other enemy soldiers to avoid the trap, or simply to locate the explosive for future retrieval, is something I will never know.

Investigation of the area around the explosion revealed it was probably a grenade triggered by a trip wire. We did find the trip wire where it had been tied to a very small bush at one end. Following the path of the trip wire, it was apparent that I had walked parallel to the wire, only inches away, for about six feet. The Sergeant had apparently stepped just a few inches to the right of my path, thus brushing the trip wire enough to detonate the booby trap. Once again, I had to wonder how I had been protected. Was it a higher guidance or just dumb luck? You probably know by now that I do not believe in luck in such situations.

Regrettably, I never heard of the wounded Sergeant again. In a way that was good because we would have been notified if he had succumbed to his wounds. I still wonder if he was crippled or otherwise disabled. I sincerely hope he was able to lead a happy and full life. He was a good trooper and had done what was asked of him.

Like so many of my troopers, I think of him often.

THE STANDOFF PATROL

The monsoon season had been with us for months. Streams were swollen, we were almost always soaked, and the mud was everywhere and on everything we touched. The warm climate helped, but we still found ourselves shivering with cold especially when on dismounted patrols. The clouds added to the gloom and made night vision almost impossible.

Our platoon was part of the squadron NDP just outside a small village. We did not trust the local villagers. There were too many instances of activity that made us certain they were feeding the Viet Cong information about us.

Late in the afternoon, I received orders to conduct a foot patrol that night. We were to move about three hundred meters down the road that ran by our NDP and the village. We would then move off the road and cross a small but swollen stream at dusk. Our movement would take us about two hundred meters further into the grassy field before us. Hopefully, we would not be observed in the darkness and would be positioned in a small rice paddy between a line of forest and the village. The intent was to intercept anyone moving between the forest and the village.

At the appointed time we set out down the road. I had approximately one half of the platoon with me and had left the other half behind to tend our fighting vehicles.

It was readily apparent, early on, that this would be an unusually difficult and dangerous mission.

We proceeded at intervals of about ten feet to allow easy maneuverability and to prevent presenting an attractive target by being grouped together. I placed the platoon sergeant, who was a seasoned veteran and had my total confidence in combat situations, near the front of the column. I located myself toward the middle of the column to allow ease of control.

After moving about one hundred meters, the difficulties began. The point man gave the hand signal to get down as he dove into the fairly deep ditch on the right hand side of the road. The ditch was filled with sharp concertina wire, as a defense for the NDP, which of course made the ditch very uncomfortable and hard to move in. As was procedure, we all followed suit immediately by diving into the ditch.

We soon learned what the problem was. The point man had seen vehicles and personnel about fifty meters ahead of us. Because of the poor visibility, he had no idea who they were since we had no knowledge of any of our friendly troops in that location. If they were friendly troops, they would probably not know who we were and if they were enemy we were in a very bad situation.

I radioed my troop commander to report the situation. He instructed me to hold our position while he tried to sort things out. After a short time, of course it seemed like an eternity, he advised me they were friendly troops from another troop, that he had advised them we were coming by their location, and ordered me to proceed with caution. Once again, lack of communication somewhere in the command chain had placed us in extreme danger.

As ordered, we proceeded and soon were at the stream crossing. The water was cold and running chest deep. We crossed one at a time with the lead elements establishing a small defensive perimeter on the other side.

As planned, it was now dark. We proceeded to the small rice paddy where we were to spend the night. Hopefully, the rain and darkness concealed our movement and exact location.

I established our perimeter in a rough half circle facing the village. Two men were placed facing the opposite direction to detect anyone approaching us from the rear. We worked in pairs to ensure at least one trooper of each pair could remain and awake and vigilant. I could not have slept if I had wanted to. The water was cold and I was continually shivering. The platoon sergeant and I were paired roughly in the middle of the perimeter line. I valued his advice and wanted him close by. For the time being, everything was quiet in our immediate area.

Sometime, around 10 P.M, we heard a massive explosion a few hundred meters beyond the village. We did not know at the time, but one of our sister platoon vehicle had hit an antitank mine constructed from a 500 pound unexploded bomb. We learned later that the force of the blast had flipped the ACAV upside down and had killed two of our troopers.

Very soon thereafter, a major firefight erupted in the vicinity of the blast. It was clear that the night that had started so ominously was quickly getting worse. The fighting went on for several hours. Judging from the volume of fire and the radio traffic I could hear on our troop radio net, our troops were engaged with a significant enemy force. Our troop commander instructed me to hold my position.

About midnight things got very interesting. We clearly heard significant movement just a few meters in front of our position. This was exactly where we expected the enemy to be if he came that night. Although we could not see them, it was clearly more soldiers than I had in my patrol.

The enemy soldiers stopped moving and took a position only a little way in front of us. I had no way of knowing whether they had detected us, or if they were positioning for the ongoing battle and waiting further orders.

The platoon sergeant agreed that we should be quiet and wait for further orders or react if necessary to an attack.

It may seem strange that the platoon sergeant and I were talking with the enemy so close. The method for talking quietly at night is to exhale slowly, place your mouth on the other person's ear, and whisper quietly. It sounds strange, but is adequate for necessary communication.

I notified the troop commander via radio using the same whisper technique except that I whispered into the radio handset rather someone's ear.

The troop commander instructed me to advise him of any changes and to hold my position. He then said something I never expected to hear. That something was very sobering. He said that because of the terrain and the fact that all our friendly troops were heavily engaged, there was little he could do to help me. We were on our own.

One can only guess why we were not attacked that night. I have to believe that the enemy knew we were there, but like us, did not know what kind or size of force confronted them.

Fortunately, after an hour or so, we could hear the enemy withdrawing.

In case anyone is foolish enough to wonder why we did not engage the enemy, no commander at any level should ever put his troops in severe peril unless it is the only way to accomplish the mission.

The remainder of the night was relatively uneventful. Eventually the ongoing battle ceased and all was quiet again.

About dawn we carefully made our way back across the stream, using a slightly different route to avoid any booby traps that might have been placed in the night, and worked our way back to the NDP.

Upon returning to the NDP, we found the mood somber. Yes, everyone was exhausted from the night's activities. More importantly, we had lost fellow troopers that night. It hurt us all whether we knew them well or not.

THE TRAILER

Somewhere not too far from Dian, the Eleventh Armored Cavalry Regiment base camp, we were moving the L Troop Headquarters to a new NDP. We were accompanied by one other platoon and the troop commander plus the troop headquarters vehicles. Third Platoon was tasked with reconnaissance and security for the troop column.

The land was generally dry and sparsely forested with scrubby native growth.

In the late morning or early afternoon, we reached a point where our path was blocked by a fairly deep gorge about thirty feet wide. The obstacle was too great for some of the headquarters wheeled vehicles to make the crossing safely.

The troop was fortunate to have, at its disposal, an M60 AVLB. The M60 AVLB is based on a M60 Patton tank chassis, but instead of the tank's gun turret, it is equipped with a bridge launcher integrated into the chassis and mounted on top. It is capable of bridging a gap up to sixty feet and will support an M60 Main Battle Tank, which weighs about sixty tons.

The M60 AVLB was quickly brought forward and deployed to span the gorge. The process of deployment took less than five minutes.

I sent several tracks across the bridge to establish security on the far side.

The first troop vehicle to attempt the crossing, other than my platoon vehicles, was the troop executive officers jeep and one-quarter ton trailer. Disaster struck just a few feet before the jeep and trailer reached the bridge. The trailer hit a mine and was absolutely destroyed.

Fortunately, we experienced no casualties and the jeep was unharmed. Only the trailer and its random contents were a total loss.

It would be fair to wonder how, with all the armored traffic that had been over the ground, was the mine not exploded before the jeep trailer set it off. I have no idea unless the narrow trailer tire placed sufficient pressure per square inch to trigger the mine where as the armored vehicles, having a very low pressure per square inch of impact on the ground, had not. Such are the mysteries of war.

We soon cleaned up the mess and continued on our mission.

The administrative after-math required ordering a replacement for the trailer and the supplies the trailer had carried. I wouldn't want to say that somebody exaggerated, but when the replacement machine gun barrels, gas cans, etc., arrived, it was apparent that several two and a half ton trucks would have been needed to carry them. It was amazing that all those supplies were destroyed in one small trailer. Troops will always find a way to have the equipment and supplies they need to survive.

DRUGS

It was the time of "flower power" at home and unfortunately a significant portion of the youth and the press chose not to support the soldiers who were making great sacrifices for them. We, of course, could not control the events at home and one would think we would be isolated from them. The drug culture was felt with great effect in the trenches.

No matter how hard the troop leaders tried, marijuana and cocaine use were rampant among the troops.

The drugs were readily available via "short time girls" and other local sources. They were supplied either at very low prices or were free. I felt then and now that the enemy made sure our troops got all the drugs they wanted. The use of drugs then and now seriously degraded the effectiveness and morale of our troops. The enemy, I am sure, knew it could do a great deal of harm by ensuring a constant and free flow of drugs.

Many times did I uncover stashes of marijuana and to the dismay of the holders, burned them on an open fire. That seemed to be more effective than other disciplinary actions that would have removed the troops, at least temporarily, from their front line duties.

I remember one young trooper in particular. He was a good soldier and frankly a valuable asset to our unit. Eventually his performance degraded and he became a liability. When I counseled him, he freely admitted he had started using marijuana and maintained that it had not affected him negatively. His degraded performance and attitude proved otherwise. I am sure that he soon graduated to the use of cocaine and became such a negative influence that I finally had to institute disciplinary action and sent him to the rear area. He had become a danger to his fellow troopers through his diminished cognitive skills and erratic behavior. He was just one of a number of young lives I saw destroyed by the "harmless" drugs.

If we were in an NDP for several days, the ground would be littered with plastic bottles used to supply the cocaine. It was a problem that did not instill a feeling a confidence in our overall combat readiness.

Let me be clear. The majority of our troopers did not use drugs nor condone their use. Still, it was a problem with which we all had to contend.

NIGHT PATROL

Night patrols were obviously necessary, but not a favorite pursuit of anyone I knew.

The mission of a night patrol was usually to interdict enemy movement along known or suspected trails. The trail might have been along an avenue of approach to one of our NDPs or simply a suspected supply route used by the VC.

The night patrol, of course, meant reduced vision making it hard to determine where the enemy might be or the size of his force. More disturbingly, it meant leaving the relative security of our armored vehicles and their immense firepower. The one advantage we could gain was that of surprise. The enemy could not see in the dark any better than we could and we hoped would stumble into our carefully designed ambush.

Another factor to us was the reality that if we became engaged in a significant fire fight, our remaining troops would most likely be deployed to come directly to our aid or form a blocking force to prevent the enemy from withdrawing safely. In either event, we knew our friendly troops might easily accidentally fire on us rather than the enemy. The darkness of night and the fog of war could easily lead to such confusion.

Preparations for a night patrol were fairly routine. I would receive the mission from the troop commander including map coordinates and any special circumstances such as location of friendly troops and any intelligence gathered on enemy force strength and movements.

Upon returning to my platoon position, I would select the appropriate patrol members, almost always including the platoon sergeant, and brief them on the mission.

The troops would be kept busy securing anything such as dog tags with tape to prevent noise from rattling. We did not have the necessary camouflage paint to diminish the shine from the oils in our skin, but we always improvised by using the soot from the exhaust pipes on our vehicles. It worked very well.

A little side-line note. My troopers seemed to get great joy from the requirement to blacken themselves with the soot. It was traditional for armored cavalry leaders to sport a moustache. I did, but it was so blonde as to be barely noticeable. The troopers loved to accuse me of requiring the soot application solely because it made my moustache easier to see. It did not bother me and I was happy they could find a little bit of good natured humor in the situation.

We would normally leave the NDP shortly before dark and intentionally take a path in a direction away from our destination. After dark we would turn and proceed to our ambush site. The idea, of course, was to deny any enemy observers the luxury of forecasting our intended ambush site.

Upon arrival at the ambush site, I would deploy the patrol in whatever defensive position maximized our fields of fire and provided all around security. The platoon sergeant was always located next to me in the event I might need his valued advice. He had a great deal more combat experience than I did. The radioman was placed close by me.

The troopers would be deployed in pairs to facilitate the buddy system. The plan was for one trooper to sleep while the other was on guard. If it sounds strange that we would sleep on patrol, please note that we had to sleep when and where we could because of the rigors of our everyday work and the often sleepless nights. Contrary to what one might think or read in comic books, it is almost impossible for any man to stare into the darkness for a long period of time and remain vigilant. If one buddy snored, the other would rouse him immediately. Under the cover of darkness, noise discipline is paramount.

Each man had his own method of seeking some comfort while being ready for instant action. We were all smart enough to be afraid for the night can be terrifying when you don't know what may happen next. My personal method, when it came my time to rest, was to lay on my back with my head toward the expected enemy avenue of approach. I could roll over onto my belly quickly if necessary and my head was close enough for the platoon sergeant to whisper in my ear if necessary. I would place my M79 grenade launcher, or my M-16 rifle, whichever I was carrying, by my side with the barrel pointed toward the enemy. My .45-caliber pistol would be placed on my chest alongside my knife. A grenade would be at the ready by my side. This may all sound a little paranoid, but I knew soldiers who had been crept up on in the darkness and had little or no time to react.

If we had not had enemy contact, then as morning approached, we would use the cover of darkness to withdraw to our NDP. We remained vigilant to ensure the enemy had not determined our presence and planned a little surprise ambush for our return trek to the NDP. Of course, a short distance before arriving at the NDP we would radio our position to ensure our fellow troopers knew we were friendlies approaching their position. The idea of being fired upon by our own armored cavalry troopers was not a pleasant thought. On one occasion we were not able to establish radio contact with the NDP. We simply stayed in place until it was light enough for our fellow troopers to recognize us. Much better safe than sorry.

Aside from the adrenaline rush of fear, night patrols are generally pretty mundane. You walk a little while in the dark, you spend the night hot and sweaty or cold and wet, and you stare into the darkness. Not exciting, but a necessary part of warfare.

PLATOON SERGEANT

Every young Second Lieutenant is told that he must listen to his platoon sergeant. In theory this is true and often good advice. After all, the platoon sergeant is usually a professional soldier and has had a great deal of experience.

One must also recognize that platoon sergeants are people and come with assets and flaws just like everyone else.

I learned the wise approach was to initially give the new platoon sergeant the benefit of the doubt and to learn where his strengths and weaknesses were prevalent.

As a platoon leader in Southeast Asia, I was fortunate to have a platoon sergeant who possessed a great deal of combat experience. While he may have been lacking in some areas, I soon learned to seek his counsel in combat situations. We might not always agree, I knew the final decision had to be mine, his experience and warrior attitude were invaluable.

I choose not to name him other than by the nickname the troopers gave him of "Bones." I never asked, but have always assumed the nickname came from something other than his tall and thin stature.

In a field environment "Bones" was a soldier's soldier. He always ensured the troopers and their equipment were ready for action. He was sometimes harsh, but he did his job. If I had to be away briefly, he would take charge of the platoon and perform whatever mission was required.

On the rare occasion that we had a few days "stand down" in a rear area, it was a different story. He would immediately disappear and go on a drunken spree until it was time for us to move on. He was usually accompanied by the First Sergeant and one or two of the other platoon sergeants.

The army rule book certainly does not condone such behavior. The truth is that the other company officers and I knew that he deserved and needed the respite.

Perhaps the following will give some insight into his behavior. "Bones was on his fourth tour as a combatant in Southeast Asia. As I mentioned before, he performed impeccably in the field environment. Yes, he was a crude man. He was a warrior at heart and had, for whatever reasons, a fierce hatred for the enemy.

On one occasion we were talking quietly. I was consciously making an effort to understand him better. He did not seem to want to talk about his life outside of the war zone, but freely related to me his one dream. His dream was to chase down a VC and cut off his ears before killing him. I knew he wasn't kidding. I don't expect anyone else to understand. I know firsthand what war can do to people.

In the end we seemed to make a great team. I learned to rely on him and respect his combat knowledge and experience. He seemed to learn to respect me and the decisions I made. This arrangement greatly enhanced our platoon's effectiveness and helped us to get our troopers home alive.

THE FIRST SERGEANTS

First Sergeants are an invaluable asset to the US Army. They are the highest ranking NCO in the company or troop and are charged with not only being the commander's liaison to the soldiers but also having many administrative and personnel duties to support the commander's plan and guidance for the unit. A good first sergeant is the commander's right hand.

I was fortunate enough to have encountered two very different first sergeants in my tour with L Troop. They were completely different individuals in leadership style and personal traits. They were both incredibly outstanding in their own way.

Upon my arrival at L Troop in Cambodia I first met First Sergeant (First Sergeants are known as Top) Montelango. He was a hard looking man and obviously a dedicated career soldier. I believe he was an American Indian, though I'm not sure, and it really does not matter then or now. He was in incredibly good shape, though small in stature. His waist was tiny for a man and his bulging chest was pure muscle. He either exercised a great deal or had a hard life. I suspect it was both. He knew his soldiers and had both their respect and fear of him.

To be fair, he was a coarse man and was prone to drink far too much. His courage before the enemy was not exceeded by any one else I knew. His judgement was not always the best, in my opinion, but he was absolutely a dedicated professional.

As I learned more about him over time, I began to understand why he was the man he was. I do not have factual evidence but was told the following by a ranking officer whom I trusted implicitly.

Top Montelango first saw combat in the Korean War. He at one point was credited with the survival of his infantry battalion. Apparently the battalion was defending a rocky ridge and was about to be overrun. The order was given to retreat, but Top stayed behind to slow the pursuing enemy at a small opening in the rocks. He was credited with shooting a number of the enemy until he ran out of ammunition. He then, because of the narrow opening was able to kill a number more with his entrenching tool. He, of course, received several wounds but his fellow soldiers were able to withdraw safely and he got away too. I was told that he was recommended for the Congressional Medal of Honor but the award was still pending. An incredible story, yes, but he was incredible man.

I also learned that when combining his Korean War experience and multiple tours in Southeast Asia, he had a number of purple hearts. Again, I saw his scars and I saw the man.

One day I asked my platoon sergeant, who was one of Top's buddies, why Top seemed to hate the VC so much. The response was that it was partly due to his experiences of several combat tours, but mostly because the VC had caused Top's son to lose both legs in S. Vietnam. Another clear clue to who the man was.

First Sergeant Cotton was in many ways completely different from First Sergeant Montelango. He was a large man in good condition and fair haired. His demeanor reminded me more of a college professor than a hardened career soldier. Make no mistake, he was a professional soldier and a good one in my opinion.

Our first meeting was early one morning. Late the night before I had moved my platoon into the troop NDP. We had been on a search-and-destroy mission for several days and were physically exhausted. The relative safety of the troop NDP was a welcome respite. Of course, we would perform required maintenance and resupply. Still, it was an opportunity for some much needed rest.

In view of the conditions, I had decided to let the troops sleep in for a couple of hours. This plan went quickly awry. I was awakened, as were my troopers, by the loud bellowing of the new First Sergeant. Of course, the troopers had no choice other than to arise and start their days. He was their First Sergeant.

Please recognize that I was accustomed to being in complete control of my platoon. I was responsible for all that they did or failed to do and was very cognizant of my need and duty to take care of them the best I could. I took my orders from the troop commander only.

Considering the fact that I was exhausted, I am sure I was not very tactful. I quickly approached the First Sergeant demanding to know who he was and why he was messing with my troopers. He, of course, replied that he was now the L Troop First Sergeant and that he was performing his duty of ensuring the troopers were doing their jobs. I informed him that they were my troopers and that if he did not like that he could take it up with the troop commander. He went back to the command track and nothing else was said at that time.

A few weeks later we had the rare pleasure of a three day "stand down" at Dian the regimental headquarters. The purpose was to give us a brief rest and more importantly to allow major maintenance and resupply. It was great because we did not have to stay up all night on guard and got three hot meals a day in the mess hall. We could even shop at the regimental post exchange.

Early in the stand down, I was approached by First Sergeant Cotton. He invited me to stop by his quarters for a game of chess and indicated he just wanted to get to know me better. I agreed.

We had an enjoyable evening. He was a well educated, sincere, and friendly man. We talked briefly about our first encounter and agreed we could have both handled the situation better. When we parted that evening we had an understanding that we were both dedicated to the welfare and discipline of the troops. We never had another problem. He performed his job in a businesslike and professional manner and proved to be totally supportive of my endeavors. He was an ideal First Sergeant whom I respected greatly.

Once again the lesson had been reinforced. "Seek to understand."

ARMORED CAVALRY
TROOP COMMANDER

Sometime in late June we were patrolling in S. Vietnam. The terrain was heavily wooded in large tracts between large open areas. The weather was hot and dry. In some ways the open areas reminded me of Fort. Hood, Texas, with the grassy plains and rolling hills.

The radio crackled with the voice of the troop radio operator who informed me that I was to take my platoon to the troop NDP immediately. I had no idea what was going on, but a return to the troop NDP had to be better than patrolling the heavily wooded areas on a search-and-destroy mission.

I was surprised to find the squadron commander at the troop NDP. Especially surprising was the apparent absence of the troop commander.

The squadron commander called me aside and informed me first that the troop commander had been flown to the rear area for reassignment. The squadron commander then informed me that I was the acting troop commander. My emotions upon hearing the news were mixed at best. They included elation, dismay, fear, and just about every other human emotion I can think of possibly experiencing.

The troop commander had been reassigned under very sad circumstances. He had been a very good and effective combat commander. He was physically large black man, therefore, stood out from the remainder of the troopers. As mentioned elsewhere, the command tracks had two antennas rather than the single antenna on the majority of tracks. His physical appearance and the antenna made him an easy target for the enemy soldiers who wanted very much to eliminate our leaders. As a result, that day his track was hit by enemy fire for the third time in the course of only a few months. Each time several of his crew members had been seriously wounded while he remained unscathed. The third time was more than he could take. The loss of his crew members and the other stresses of combat leadership apparently pushed him past his personal limit. I saw him at regimental HQ a few weeks later and was shocked at his demeanor. He appeared to be a shell of the man to whom I owed so much. His leadership had been instrumental in enabling me to be an effective platoon leader.

The squadron commander was kind enough to make me aware of a potential problem in his appointment of me as acting troop commander. Another platoon leader in our troop was a West Point Academy graduate. He was an outstanding officer and I believe eventually rose to the rank of Major General. The problem was that he had been in country only a short time, but technically, he outranked me by one day. It was common practice at the time to delay date of rank for non–West Point graduates to ensure the West Point graduates had date of rank advantage. The squadron commander had discussed the situation with the other platoon leader and they agreed that I was the better choice. I am sure there were repercussions from higher levels, but the squadron commander told me that was his problem. I will always feel admiration for the other lieutenant. He put the well being of the unit first over something that would have enhanced his personal status.

Before leaving, the squadron commander gave me orders to move the troop to a position several kilometers away. That story is related herein under the section entitled "Short Time Girls."

Well, I had wondered what it was like to be a troop commander. I would probably not have chosen a combat role as the environment to learn how to be a troop commander, but that is how life happens sometimes. I was officially the "Old Man," the common term among troops for the commander. I did not feel like the "Old Man" since I was only twenty four years of age. Of course, the vast majority of my troopers were even younger than I.

The first night was fortunately uneventful for the troop. I spent most of the early evening in the command track listening to situation reports and familiarizing myself with the locations of the troop's platoons and ensuring the support sections were ready for the next day.

Just before dusk, the troop First Sergeant asked me to follow him. I did not know what he needed, but he had my full confidence. He escorted me to a large tent in the middle of the troop NDP. The tent was empty except for a cot in the middle. I knew, of course, that this was the troop commander's personal tent. I quickly thanked the First Sergeant and told him that I was only in command temporarily and preferred to sleep on my track with the platoon. He very clearly and respectfully informed me that the troopers viewed me as the troop commander and they expected me to fill the role in all matters. I understood what he was saying and thanked him for his candor.

The first night sleeping alone in the tent was not a fun experience. I had learned sometime before that the commander I was replacing had been seriously wounded in that environment on a previous tour. The enemy had infiltrated the troop position and, of course, knew they would likely find the leader in that tent. I slept like I would have on a ground patrol. My .45-caliber pistol was in firing mode laying on my chest and my knife was out of the sheath by my side. Being the commander can be very lonely and scary.

The next morning I issued the necessary directives to the combat platoon leaders and spent most of the day monitoring their progress.

Shortly after sunset on the second day, one of our platoons became heavily engaged in a firefight. I immediately ordered another platoon to a position closer to the platoon engaged in the fight. I immediately notified the squadron commander. He informed me that he had been monitoring my radio traffic and would continue to do so. He calmed my nerves by telling me he was there to support and advise me as necessary. It was nice to know I was not alone when the stakes were so high.

The battle was soon over. We did have to medevac one trooper with bullet wounds. The remainder of the night was quiet.

I do not remember exactly how long I was acting troop commander but I believe it was only a few days. I was happy to return
to my platoon when the new company commander arrived. The
experience had been awesome, but I was more comfortable with my
old platoon.

THE INFANTRY CAPTAIN

It had been another long platoon level search-and-destroy mission. We were tired but happy for it was our time to return to the troop NDP for a day. We were looking forward to a good hot meal, refueling and maintenance of our vehicles, replenishing ammunition, and maybe just a little rest.

As we entered the NDP area, the first order of business was to refuel our vehicles and move them to the NDP perimeter for security. The men all knew that when that was done, they could go get a hot meal and then attend to the other maintenance and resupply issues.

Almost immediately upon arriving at the NDP I received a radio message directing me to report to the troop commander. Upon reporting I saw an infantry captain who without further explanation, introduced himself as the new troop commander. It seems that someone in higher headquarters thought it would be a good opportunity for him to cross train in a different branch of the Army.

My thoughts were immediately wary, but a soldier does as he is directed.

Without hesitation he ordered me to move my platoon to a site a few kilometers from the NDP. I told him that I would do so as soon as we were able to refuel. He then screamed at me to move them immediately and I protested that we could not fight effectively without fuel. He screamed at me again that I would proceed to the new location as soon as we refueled. I then asked him for a concept of the mission. I obviously needed to know what the mission consisted of if we were to accomplish the mission. He screamed that I would find out when I got there and ordered me out of his sight.

It was not a fun task telling my troopers that we had to move immediately and especially since I could not even tell them why.

I was very disturbed by our encounter, but I knew had to obey orders even if they did not make good sense to me.

We soon arrived at our designated position and quickly set up a defensive perimeter in the edge of a wooded area overlooking an open field several hundred yards across. I reported my position to the troop commander. Once again I was totally surprised when he ordered me to move the platoon to the middle of the field and to place them in a line formation. I did so and reported to the troop commander once again. He told me to have troopers return to the wood line and cut enough brush to camouflage the vehicles in the middle of the field. He added that this was good training and that he was going to "whip us into shape." Having no choice, I ordered my platoon to comply with the troop commander's directives. They were not happy about being in an exposed position for no apparent reason. They had proven over time that they would do whatever it took to accomplish the mission without hesitation. This circumstance, however, seemed to defy all reason.

I was in a tough spot. I had to obey orders, but I also had to support and protect my troopers.

I quickly made a decision that I knew could destroy my career, but it had to be done.

I called the squadron commander on the radio and briefly explained my predicament. I knew the troop commander would be monitoring the squadron radio net and would hear everything I said. Fortunately, the squadron commander had great faith in me and knew I would not take such an action without good reason. The squadron commander instructed me to move my platoon into a defensive position and await his arrival.

It wasn't long before the squadron commander arrived in his helicopter to talk with me. Of course, I was worried, but I related the situation to him as best I could. He told me to hold my position and to await further orders from him.

An hour or so later, the squadron executive officer radioed to order my platoon to return the troop NDP.

Upon our arrival at the troop NDP, I found the squadron commander was still there. To my relief, the new troop commander was not there. The squadron commander took me aside and told me the problem had been resolved. Nothing else was said, but I knew the reputation of our platoon had saved us, especially me, on that occasion.

We spent the remainder of the day in the troop NDP and went on to future missions as directed.

It is not my intention to belittle any combat branch whatsoever. The officer involved in this event happened to be infantry. I will never understand his actions, but let me be clear that I have known many officers in a variety of branches who were highly effective and dedicated in their military pursuits.

A combat leader faces many challenges. In order to be effective, he must be loyal to his soldiers and the mission no matter what the cost may be to him personally. Doing the right thing is an absolute imperative.

RATS

The life of a soldier is often vastly different from that to which he is accustomed in the good old USA.

The showers, a comfortable bed, air conditioning, an ice box, and so many other simple conveniences are not available to the combat soldier.

The places we found ourselves were often squalid with standing water, knee deep mud, insects, etc. This was especially true of positions previously held by ARVN or other US Troops. It was a fact of life that heavy occupancy of a small area in a jungle environment would soon result in a less than desirable piece of real estate.

Of all the problems inherent to such areas, the one that bothered me and many of my fellow soldiers the most, was the ever present horde of rats.

I never knew of anyone to be bitten by the rats, but by their very nature they are nasty little creatures and are to be avoided whenever possible.

My personal disgust for the vermin was brought home forcefully to me one night. We were occupying an existing NDP somewhere near Xuan Loc. The site was disgusting, but that was where we ordered to stay. It was my turn to sleep on the ammo cans on the bottom of our track. As usual, I pulled a light poncho liner over myself and proceeded to sleep the best I could.

Sometime, in the early morning hours, I experienced a bad dream. The dream was centered around two rats fighting on my chest. Unfortunately, I awoke to find two large rats fighting on my chest. My immediate reaction, of course, was to get them off of me. If you want to fault me for acting like a wild man, imagine yourself in that situation. There was a real element of danger in the situation. Of course, my antics awakened the other sleeping crew members and got the attention of the crewman on guard in the cupola. In the dark, none of them knew what was happening. The first thing to come to mind was the possibility that an enemy soldier was in the track with us and that I was trying to fight him off. Believe me, a track full of soldiers awakened so rudely and all with guns at the ready to fight the unknown threat is not to be taken lightly. I was able to make everyone understand what was really happening before any of us got killed.

If you are expecting some pearl of wisdom about jungle fighting, I have none other than to point out that a soldier's sacrifice is manifested in many ways.

Let it be known that I still hate rats.

THE OER

As in any business, every soldier is rated by his superiors on his performance from time to time. For officers, the official document is the Officer Efficiency Report (OER). As in most rating systems, the numbers are often inflated in order to support the officer's career potential. A poor OER is almost always the death knell for a career.

After several months in country it was time for me to receive a periodic OER. It was written by my troop commander and endorsed by the squadron commander.

I knew I had done my best and was pleased to see a high score and a glowing report from the troop commander. It was with amazement that I read the squadron commander's endorsement. It was a glowing report, the most significant portion of which was written in less than stellar English but definitely made the point. It read, "This officer never failed to accomplish the mission." That report was, of course, a high point of my day and a tremendous morale booster. I knew my purpose in being there was to "accomplish the mission."

I write of this not to be boastful. I knew I had not been able to accomplish anything alone. My troopers and all our support staff and troops made it possible.

Everyone who cares about their job wants to do it well and to be acknowledged by others. This only increased my resolve to be the best officer I could be in every instance. I knew then and now that I could not be perfect. I could only strive to do my best.

HAND AND ARM SIGNALS

There are a multitude of tasks that are critical to the successful leadership of a combat unit. It is difficult to single out one task as the most important because they are all building blocks required to make the unit function. Failure in any of the tasks can easily result in mission failure, which is absolutely unacceptable. You seldom get do-overs in a combat situation.

One of the required tasks is, obviously, adequate communication. The troopers have to understand what is happening and what is expected of them in order to perform as an effective team.

When possible, face-to-face communication is ideal. This may be accomplished in mission briefings and sometimes during breaks in action.

In reality, armored units are deployed with some distance between vehicles and are often separated by terrain and foliage. The noise and confusion of battle add to the difficulty.

Fortunately, we were blessed with radios on each vehicle, two on the platoon leaders' and platoon sergeants' vehicles, and intercom systems within the individual armored vehicles.

The platoon leader and platoon sergeant were required to monitor the higher headquarters radio net, give direction and receive information on the platoon radio net, and interact as necessary on their individual vehicle intercom. The traffic on each radio net could be heard through the CVC (combat vehicle commander helmet) and outgoing communication was available by flipping a switch on the CVC to enter the desired radio net. This, of course, required thought and coordination, but was a fairly workable system even with all the other tasks that required our attention.

Unfortunately, our radio systems were designed and manufactured by human beings and I suspect were provided by the lowest bidder on the government contract. It was not at all unusual to have several armored vehicles operating without working radios. At one time, none of my vehicles had an operating radio.

Needless to say, I was not always able to direct the platoon through radio communication and verbal communication was not an option while we were on the move or in an active firefight.

Before I left for Southeast Asia, several people told me to "keep my head down." Sounds like a good idea, but not always possible in combat.

On numerous occasions I had to rely on hand and arms signals to direct the platoon movement and placement of fires. Often the only way to be seen was to stand on top of my vehicle in order to be seen by the various elements of my platoon. It does not require a deep thinker to recognize that the enemy could also see me clearly and I knew that they would love to "take me out" since I was the "leader."

Why would I do such an obviously stupid thing? It was my job! The only way to accomplish the mission, and get as many of us as possible home safely, was to direct the operation as best I could. Failure to communicate was not an option.

FREEDOM BIRDS

Another patrol somewhere near Xuan Loc. The days were generally hot and dry. The low lying areas and the heavily trafficked areas were still soft and full of stagnant water from the rainy season. The rats and mosquitoes seemed to love the climate.

For several days, our platoon performed limited search-and-destroy missions during the daylight hours and then established a platoon night defensive position a few kilometers from Bien Hoa Air Force Base. The area was fairly flat with lots of tall grass and some forested areas.

Bien Hoa AFB was a point of embarkation to and from South Vietnam. We all dreamed of the day when it would be our turn to go there and catch a flight, we called them "Freedom Birds," to the great PX, otherwise known as home.

We would usually arrive at our NDP site several hours before dark. There was limited enemy activity, since we departed Cambodia only a few weeks before. It took the enemy at least a few months to rebuild and resupply from the damage we had caused to them in Cambodia.

I was never told why we were patrolling that specific area. I always felt it was a level of security for the nearby AFB.

Once we were in our NDP, there was little to be done other than rest, eat, perform minor maintenance, and of course, remain vigilant for enemy activity. We could never assume that we were in a position of safety.

Every evening, shortly before dark, a Freedom Bird would depart from Bien Hoa and fly rather low over our position as it made its ascent on the journey home. It was easy to recognize them as Freedom Birds as they were chartered commercial Airliners.

As I would watch the Freedom Bird fly over us, I noticed that all the platoon members were doing the same thing. I would daydream of what it would be like to be a passenger on that aircraft and, of course, hoped the day would come soon.

The boredom of guard duty, even in daylight, can cause the mind to have strange thoughts.

Sometimes, I would become overwhelmed with jealousy. Why was it their turn and not mine? Of course, I would quickly regain my senses and be glad that at least somebody was getting to go home. I knew that most, if not all, of the soldiers on that aircraft had paid their dues.

Soon the Freedom Bird would climb out of sight. Time to get back to the business of war.

THE VIPS

We had been back to South Vietnam for several weeks and were glad to be out of Cambodia. It was still a war zone, but the constant threat of attack seemed to have lessened.

The squadron NDP was similar to the others we had established. The trash, dirt berm, mud, and rats were the same.

Our uniforms were tattered and we were not looking very sharp as troops normally do. It is hard to look sharp when you are covered with mud or dust and have no way to shower. I am sure we did not smell very good, but we were all in the same condition so it was not noticeable to us.

One afternoon several Huey helicopters arrived at our location. They did get our attention as they were transporting the regimental commander, several of his staff officers, and to our surprise a few civilians.

We were, of course, curious, but continued with our duties as is appropriate for soldiers, especially in a combat environment.

The visitors were in the headquarters tent for a while, I assumed for a briefing. When they emerged, our squadron commander led them to my position and approached me. The squadron commander introduced us. The regimental commander I recognized, but was surprised to learn the civilians included two United States senators and a high-level delegation from General Motors Corporation.

The group was on an inspection tour and were specifically concerned with the Sheridan Tanks we used. They soon asked for my opinion of the Sheridan Tank.

Considering the high ranking status of the delegation, and the presence of the regimental commander, I was a little intimidated. Well, maybe a lot intimidated. I knew however, as a good officer, I had to be honest and render the truth.

I related the following opinions.

The Sheridan Tank was an awesome fighting vehicle. It's relatively lightweight worked well in our terrain. The track system was very effective and seldom failed in contrast to the heavier M60A1 tanks. The firing systems were very effective especially in view of the fléchette rounds we deployed against personnel on the ground. The fléchette rounds spewed thousands of small darts that would clear foliage and certainly eliminate any enemy soldiers unlucky enough to be on the receiving end of the rounds.

It was apparent, at this point, that the delegation was pleased with what I had to say. Especially the General Motors Corporation representatives.

The smiles quickly faded as I related the rest of the story.

The Sheridan had several weaknesses, in my view. If hit in a vulnerable spot, they tended to burn furiously and explode. A small seal in the main gun would sometimes fail, resulting in the inability to fire the main gun. The type of charge used in the main gun left a heavy residue in the barrel, which required swabbing, sometimes even when we were in a firefight. The worst problem seemed to be a mismatch between the turbo engine and the transmission. It seemed that replacing the engine soon resulted in a failure of the transmission. Likewise, replacement of the transmission seemed to result in failure of the engine.

It may seem like a lot of problems, but overall I would take Sheridans into combat anytime anywhere. They did the job.

Noting the displeasure of the delegation, the Regimental Commander quickly thanked me for my candor, and led the delegation to another area of the NDP.

Perhaps it wasn't the best thing for me to have given such an honest opinion. It was, however, the right thing to do. Those people were the ones in a position to improve our equipment. Our lives and the lives of future soldiers would depend in part on their actions.

I will always believe the Regimental Commander truly did appreciate my candor. He was a great leader and later rose to the rank of Lieutenant General. He was wise enough to understand his troopers knew the equipment better than the engineers and politicians.

ARVN

The soldiers of the Army of the Republic of Vietnam were, of course, our allies in the Area of Operations.

We fully recognized that we were invited guests in their country. We welcomed their help in most cases.

Working with the ARVN soldiers was sometimes problematic.

The language barrier was a minor problem that could usually be overcome through the use of interpreters.

The real challenge was in knowing whom we could and could not trust. Unfortunately, we had to believe that the ARVN ranks had been infiltrated by enemy soldiers. In some cases, we were proven to be correct in that belief.

Overall, I personally found the ARVN soldiers to be dedicated and good allies. As in all things, some were exceptional, and some were not.

My observation was that they were generally brave and could be depended on to do their part.

They had to learn to trust us, just as we had to learn to trust them. One particular occasion brought that point home to me. We received a mission to establish our platoon NDP at a position on a known enemy trail. Our intelligence community had information that a large group of enemy soldiers would be using that trail on that evening.

An ARVN infantry company was assigned to accompany us. It was obviously the first time they had ever deployed with an armored cavalry unit.

Upon arriving at the position, the ARVN company commander began deploying his troops on the ground between our tracks. Through the use of our interpreter, I explained to him that he needed to deploy his troops in a semicircle about one hundred feet in front of our tracks to provide early warning of approaching enemy troops. He refused to do so, stating that he needed the protection of our heavy weapons and did not want to be accidently fired on by our tracks. I understood his fears, but that did not alter the requirements of the mission.

I had no choice other than to report the situation to my troop commander. He, in turn, went to his commander, who I assume talked with the ARVN higher commander.

Soon the ARVN company received a radio message through his command channel instructing him to perform the mission as I outlined it. He quickly moved his soldiers to the proper positions. At his request, I sent my interpreter with him to relay any urgent messages.

Let me be very clear. I would not want to position myself or my troopers in front of an armored cavalry platoon with its awesome firepower. Effective tactics, however, sometimes require unpleasant actions.

SURPRISE ENCOUNTER

As we ran a mid-day patrol along a tree line a few hundred meters from our squadron NDP, we felt we were having an easy day. The sun was shining and we could hear children playing in the small village not far away.

We were never totally at ease. Even though we did not expect to encounter any major situations so close to the NDP, it was possible we could stumble across booby traps or even a small unit of VC preparing a rocket or mortar attack on the NDP.

The area had been mostly cleared and we came to a halt in a small clearing with large trees and undergrowth around it. I placed the platoon in a defensive circle and we waited there for a short time. I do not recall the reason we had been halted.

One of the troopers, for some reason known only to him and God, decided to walk outside of our small perimeter and behind a tree. He had to relieve himself and I suppose just wanted a little privacy for a change.

After only a few moments we heard a loud yell and saw him furiously running and pointing behind him as he ran to his track. We soon learned that he had encountered a young man wearing only shorts and sandals. The man he met was as surprised as our trooper and immediately ran into the underbrush. He must have been deaf to not have known we were there. A platoon of armored cavalry is not exactly quiet as it moves through the brush or anywhere else for that matter.

Our normal reaction would be to open fire immediately. That was not a good option in this case. Our NDP was only a few hundred meters away and would have been the recipient of many of our outgoing rounds.

We were not receiving incoming fire, therefore I dispatched two ground patrols to scout our immediate area. We did not find the young man or any evidence that anyone else had been there recently. We did, however, find something very disconcerting.

The search revealed a small bunker, more like a deep foxhole, that the VC we had encountered had obviously occupied for some time. There were a few empty c ration cans and a small supply of spoiled food. It was apparent that he had been hiding very closely under our noses and had been reporting on our squadron NDP activities. We did not find a radio, but we assumed, had been adjusting rocket and mortar fires on our NDP.

Yes, our trooper was lax in going outside of the perimeter. We were glad to find the enemy soldier and at least deprive him of his vantage point.

One never knows from moment to moment what strange things will happen in a combat zone.

THE MARSH PATROL

We were once again on a search-and-destroy mission. The day was hot, and the terrain was muddy because of recent rains. We were operating about two kilometers from our troop NDP near Xuan Loc.

The terrain consisted of a very large grassy plain with a deep drop off to our right that quickly became a marshy area with a lot of forest. The marsh obviously would not support our armored vehicles. To our dismay, that meant another ground patrol.

We circled our tracks in an easily defendable area and prepared for the dismounted patrol. I ordered two troopers from each track to prepare. The patrol I planned would be less than a kilometer in length; therefore, each trooper took only water and his personal weapon plus a few grenades. I had learned to carry my driver's M79 Grenade Launcher with shotgun ammunition. It was short range, but devastating in close quarters such as brush.

It was obvious that we would be out of sight of our tracks and would not have their support if things turned bad.

As we descended down a slope about one hundred meters to the marsh, I had my radio man perform checks to ensure I had communication with my tracks and the troop commander.

We soon arrived at the edge of a large clearing a few hundred yards across. It was a few inches deep in water and devoid of any significant vegetation. That presented a dilemma. Normally I would send my patrol through the edge of the wood line for cover and concealment. That was not an option in this scenario.

Our only choice seemed to be to cross the open terrain without cover and concealment.

I requested that our troop commander establish preplanned mortar fire to cover the far side of the clearing. The troop commander agreed and instructed me to stay in close contact with him.

My plan for crossing the clearing was to leave half of my troops in the tree line to provide covering fire if needed. The remainder of my patrol would cross the clearing basically in pairs forming a long line with wide intervals. I did not want a group to make a tempting target. Because of the nature of the mission, I joined the troopers crossing the exposed area.

We were about half way across the clearing when I felt it. That sixth-sense feeling was very intense. I immediately halted the crossing and ordered my troopers into a prone position. I then called the troop commander and appraised him of my intense feeling. He knew my troopers and I would do whatever was necessary. He also had observed my actions enough to trust my instincts. He ordered us to return to our tracks immediately. When I advised him that we were out of the clearing, he requested a155M Howitzer barrage on the area across the clearing where we had preplanned mortar fires. That should have deterred, if not destroyed, any enemy troops in that area.

Sometimes, it is necessary to deviate from plans. My sixth-sense had never failed me before and I am certainly glad the troop commander had confidence in me. The mission was accomplished and my troopers were alive. What more could I ask for?

VISITING WOUNDED

During my tenure as Troop Commander, I had the pleasure, at the direction of the Squadron Commander, of visiting the troop's sick and wounded in the field hospital at Bien Hoa AFB near Saigon.

Although none of them had been wounded on my watch, they were all my men and I truly cared about them. Of course, I could do little or nothing for them except to reassure them that their Armored Cavalry family did care about them. We engaged in small talk and I know I left more blessed than them.

A couple of events occurred while I was at the hospital. One event was pleasant and the other devastating to me.

The pleasant event happened when I was about to go through a door inside the hospital. The door suddenly swung open almost knocking me to the ground. As I recovered my balance, I saw a huge man with Lieutenant Colonel Insignia. He was in a hurry and was closely followed by three or four ARVN. To my surprise, it was the officer I had known as Major Matthews. He had been my de facto mentor during my ROTC training at Oklahoma State University. He had been very demanding of me, but, was absolutely always there when I needed help. I owe a great deal to him. Upon recognizing me he noted my rank of first lieutenant and brusquely asked me what I was doing. I quickly explained that I was an acting armored cavalry troop commander and was visiting our troops. He smiled and said good job or words to that effect before quickly proceeding about his business.

The other event was not so pleasant. As I was reading a list of patients on a bulletin board, I was surprised to see the name of my first troop commander at Fort Hood, Texas. He was not a person that was near and dear to me. Nevertheless, I knew I should visit him if possible. He was in a critical care section of the hospital. I asked a nurse if I might see him and she indicated I could when I told her I knew him. He was severely wounded but did recognize me and was able to mutter a few words before surprisingly holding my hand in his. As I was leaving, the nurse approached me and revealed his status to me. He had, after leaving Fort Hood, become a Cobra Attack Helicopter Pilot. That morning he was on a close support strafing mission and had been shot down. Along with many other injuries his back was broken. The nurse told me that he would probably not live through the day and that they were just trying to make him comfortable. She then broke, what I thought was my combat hardened heart, when she told me that his first child, a little girl, had been born that morning and that he most likely would never see his daughter. I thanked the nurse for sharing with me and went back to hold his hand for just a few more minutes although I don't think he knew I had returned. I was in a hurry, but some things just have to be done.

I soon found a helicopter ride back to L Troop Headquarters. The visit to the hospital that day remains vivid in my memory to this day.

HHT COMMANDER FORWARD

Following many months on line as a platoon leader, the squadron commander decided to assign me to a new role. I was still performing well, but my physical condition was deteriorating and it was customary to eventually assign leaders to new roles where their experience could be well utilized and their personal resumes enhanced in support of their career progression. Also, much like air crew serving in the European Theater in World War II, a large number of missions was deemed to entitle the individual to a work in a little bit safer environment.

The US Army Table of Organization does not include the title of Headquarters and Headquarters Troop Commander Forward. I was given the official position of HHT Executive Officer. In view of our circumstance, which required the HHT Commander's full attention to his many duties at the Regimental Fire Base, I was assigned the duties of HHT Commander at the Squadron Fire Base in the field, hence being known as the HHT Commander Forward.

My responsibilities entailed overseeing all the support troops at the Squadron Firebase. The areas included resupply, maintenance, armament, medical services, administration, and any incidental requirements to support the squadron.

I was very fortunate to have outstanding noncommissioned officers directing the efforts in all the support areas. They worked hard and understood the importance of their missions.

I sometimes felt guilty as it did not seem I was really needed. All I really had to do was ensure my people were aware of mission status and receive daily reports on what they were doing and what they needed to support their efforts. Of course, I would do my best to assist them if they were having trouble getting what they needed to perform.

At the end of each day, I would brief the Squadron Commander on the status of our support missions. It was not a difficult task and I did realize that the Squadron Commander had to understand the status and readiness capabilities of his troops and vehicles.

Additionally, I had responsibility for perimeter security of the Squadron NDP. The troops on the perimeter were experienced and knew what to do. I would still walk the perimeter in the late evening just be sure something had not been overlooked.

The NDP was always a busy place. A lot of helicopters ferried troops and resupply to our position daily. Maintenance and resupply efforts seemed to be never ending.

It certainly was not a vacation, but my life was easier. I initially shared a tent with several of the staff officers and got to sleep on a real cot. Eventually, my NCOs did me a great favor. They somehow found a small covered trailer and provided it for me as my personal quarters. It was very thoughtful of them, but it left me alone, was hot, and was far too exposed to incoming shellings. It shook violently when our 155 Howitzers were firing and was infested with rats. Of course, I said nothing and accepted the gift graciously. It would have been wrong and poor leadership to deny the NCOs of the pleasure of giving. Even so, the nights were not constantly interrupted by radio messages and guard duty. It was a nice change and certainly was good for my general health.

Unfortunately, the busy NDP was a lucrative target for enemy gunners. We had to be prepared for mortar and rocket fire at any time. We had bunkers prepared, but the enemy shellings were often far too successful resulting in heavy casualties among our troopers.

My tenure as HHT Commander must have been successful. As we were preparing to stand down, since the unit was being deactivated, the NCOs really warmed my heart. They presented me with a small gift and very ceremoniously saluted and thanked me for my leadership. That gesture was not expected or required of them and will always be a great memory for me.

THE BARREL

Another late afternoon as HHT forward commander at the wasteland NDP we temporarily called home. The weather was hot and dry. Generally better than the monsoon season.

The day had been rather uneventful, filled with the normal briefings and other daily tasks, I was sitting in my tent reading a book and enjoying a little quiet time. I was temporarily alone and found the moment to be peaceful and relaxing.

The silence was shattered instantly with the sounds of explosions and screams of "incoming." It was yet another rocket and mortar attack on our position.

I immediately dove into a small bunker we had constructed in one corner of the tent I shared with three other officers. The bunker was shallow and covered with half sections of corrugated metal piping. Sandbags topped the bunker.

The time in the bunker was probably the most terrifying of all my experiences in the combat zone. There is something about being alone in such situations that heightens one fear. Of course, all I could do was lie there and wait for the shelling to stop and pray my bunker did not take a direct hit.

As soon as the shelling stopped I ran to the perimeter where it was obvious we had taken casualties. Pistol in hand, we never knew if VC had made it into the perimeter, I approached the prone figure of a young trooper. He was face down so I turned him over as gently as I could to evaluate his condition. He had an immense number of shrapnel wounds throughout his head and body. It was obviously beyond my capabilities to render aid to him so I simply cradled him in my arms and screamed for a medic.

We suffered a significant number of wounded. The wounded were all moved to the center of the NDP near the medic's track where our lone medic did a fantastic job of performing triage and tending to those he could help.

Naturally I was very concerned about the trooper I had tried to help. I saw that he had been lain about twenty feet from the others and did not seem to be getting any attention. I questioned the medic about him and was very tactfully informed that the trooper had succumbed to his wounds. It was a shock to me but there was nothing any of us could do to alter the situation.

Soon a large flight of helicopters arrived to evacuate our wounded to the field hospital.

It was my job to inspect the perimeter to ensure we were still secure. As I did so, I wondered why we had taken so many casualties. The incoming fire had been incredibly accurate.

I was able to discover one devastating factor. It was common practice when we were to occupy an NDP for an extended time, to place a few 55 gallon metal drums around the perimeter for the purpose of burning our trash. After all, it was difficult to maintain any sense of sanitation in those conditions. It was undoubtedly pure luck, but one of the incoming rounds had landed in one of the metal drums. The shrapnel from the drum was devastating to anyone nearby. I ordered the remaining barrels removed and small pits to be dug in which we could collect and burn our trash.

A few days later we discovered the reason the enemy had been able to obtain such accuracy in their attack.

We had established a three-seater outhouse on one side of the NDP. The waste would be collected in metal barrels cut in half and then as needed would be soaked in diesel fuel and burned. The system was effective and relatively sanitary. The problem was that we hired a local to burn the barrels. One afternoon, a trooper noticed the local pacing off various distances to locations within the NDP. By using the three-seater as a reference point, the enemy gunners were able to place their projectiles very accurately by knowing the exact distances to the target. The local was relinquished to the South Vietnamese Army for trial and punishment. I'm sure he was not happy with the outcome. I did not care. Another enemy taken care of. Besides, no matter what the local's fate, it did not change the devastation to which he had contributed.

PEANUTS

In my tenure as HHT commander forward I generally stayed at the Squadron NDP and had the pleasure of being around many of the squadron staff officers.

This was a pleasing relief to me for after the lonely life of a platoon leader, I was ready to make friends and have conversations with my cohorts.

One very special friend was a Lieutenant named David Wood. David was a man of very small stature and frankly many people would consider him to be a bit nerdy.

His position was that of Squadron Civil Affairs Officer. His duties required that he basically coordinate with the local population and if possible gain their support. A nearly impossible job from which he did not shrink.

David was liked by all I knew, but seemed to be closer to me than most. I enjoyed his company after a long day of work and we would sometimes talk for hours about home and whatever else young soldiers find interesting.

One fond memory gave us both a great laugh. It was shortly after midnight and after we had endured a significant mortar and rocket attack. As was the standard practice, we had both left our shelters and were carefully working our way through the NDP looking for wounded soldiers or VC sappers who may have slipped in during the attack. The sappers would tend to creep into our positions and place large explosive bags on key positions.

As I turned a corner around a track, there was David. Please remember he had just arisen from an effort to get some sleep. He had his forty-five pistol drawn. He was adorned in a combat helmet, baggy fatigue shirt unbuttoned, underwear, and unlaced boots. The attire along with his slight stature made it a very comical sight. We looked at each other for a moment and then simultaneously broke into laughter. A moment that only friends could truly savor.

I respected David greatly. He wanted to be a combat leader, but knew that would not be his lot in life. He did his job to the best of his ability.

As we would talk, I learned a little bit about his life back in the "world" as we called the USA. He had no family other than an aunt who had basically raised him. I believe his home was in S. Carolina. He held a master's degree and was proud to announce that the subject of his master's thesis was "Peanuts" the comic strip. That fit him so well.

Eventually our Squadron was deactivated and we were sent our separate ways. I had no further contact with David and frankly thought of him often.

I had been home from Southeast Asia for sometime when my father handed me a letter. It was from David's aunt. She had found my home address among David's personal effects. She informed me that he had been assigned as an advisor to an ARVN combat unit. On his last mission he was riding in a Chinook helicopter ferrying the ARVN troops on an insertion mission. The helicopter was shot down and all aboard were killed. Needless to say, the news struck me hard. I still think of David quite frequently. He, like so many others, did not have a chance to have a family and all the other good things of a long life. He was a trooper and did what had to be done.

THANKSGIVING DAY

Yes, Virginia, holidays do occur in combat zones.

I had held the position of Squadron Headquarters and Headquarters Troop (HHT) Commander Forward for over a month; therefore, I was located at the Squadrons NDP in the field. We had been in the same position for several weeks.

The days and nights were filled with briefings and the various duties of ensuring the squadron troops received the logistical support they needed to function. There was, of course, the occasional enemy rocket attack to break the boredom.

The holiday was really not a great deal different from any other day in the field. We did, however, make an effort to make it special. Routine patrols were suspended and the helicopter boys delivered a hot thanksgiving meal that was not anything like Moms', but was enjoyed anyway.

In the afternoon, we organized a volleyball game in the center of the NDP. Of course, we ensured perimeter security was intact.

The men were enjoying the game and even invited me to play. Of course, I did my best, but had to rely on the real athletes for the tough situations.

The game had been in progress for a few minutes when we were reminded of where we were. A brief rocket and mortar barrage came our way. I guess the enemy was jealous because we were obviously having a good time. Fortunately, we did not suffer any casualties.

After a short time required to have a helicopter visually recon the area and to allow our gunners to reload, we resumed the volleyball game. Yes, we were a little on edge, but we still had a good time.

Not too exciting, but that was our holiday in S. Vietnam.

CHRISTMAS MASS

The holidays are always a tough time for soldiers. Although they are probably among friends, it is just not the same as being with loved ones on those special days.

Christmas was especially difficult for me. Although I knew I would be leaving on Christmas day for R and R (rest and relaxation) in Hawaii for a whole week where I would see Mom and Dad and my, at that time, girlfriend. I longed for the memories of the wonderful Christmas times of past days. A special meal in the field and the occasional gifts the helicopter pilots would drop off to us were great, but just not the same.

I was HHT (Headquarters Troop) forward commander at Christmas time and no longer routinely went on patrols. The work was still plentiful, living conditions marginal, and of course, frequent incoming enemy fire.

On Christmas Eve, the squadron chaplain, whom I had befriended, invited me to Christmas Mass in his tent. He was a very good man and a Catholic priest. He had a way of placing himself on the same level of any trooper. His true caring and ability to work with almost any trooper made him a great asset and a tremendous morale booster.

The time approached for the Mass and I walked toward the Chaplain's tent. Raised as a good Baptist boy I had no experience with the Catholic faith other than a few Catholic friends in high school. I entered with some trepidation but was comforted by knowing the good chaplain would not embarrass anyone and would give us guidance if we felt uneasy.

The Chaplain's tent was much like our quarters. A cot occupied one corner and a small one or two man bunker was in the corner. Of course, the floor was dirt, or mud depending on the season, and the only light was from a small electric lantern. The chaplain even had a Christmas tree similar to the one we had made in our tent. It was a scraggly brown tree branch with a few beer cans hung from string for decoration. Not fancy, but the thought was well intended.

My fears were not well founded. Only three of my fellow Lieutenants and one Captain attended. As he was about to start the service, the chaplain thanked us for coming and recognizing he was one of the two Catholics in attendance said he would use the short version of the Mass and assured us we were welcome.

The Chaplain began and we were all striving to be reverent. In the circumstances, being reverent meant we were quiet and our weapons were in safety lock. Not meant to be funny, just the way it was.

After no more than three minutes, the Chaplain said Amen and announced the service was concluded. He was a man of his word. I know he did not shortcut the Mass to be disrespectful, but instead was reaching out to us in yet another way.

As we started to leave, he ask us to linger saying he had a present for us. Reaching under his cot, he pulled out what I believe was a large ammo can. Opening the can, he revealed beer and soda and offered it to us. He also had a bottle of liquor for those who wished to partake. We all stayed for about an hour and had a great time just relaxing and laughing for a change.

It was a wonderful Christmas Eve.

R AND R

Rest and Relaxation tours (R and R) were a welcome respite from the rigors of war. Unlike soldiers in most previous wars, we were rewarded with a one week vacation during our tour. There were several destinations from which we could choose. I chose Hawaii. We paid for our own lodging and meals, but the government flew us to our destination.

It was my good fortune to arrange for my parents and then girlfriend to join me on my R and R, which started officially the day after Christmas. Needless to say, having been in the combat theater of operations since May, I was ready for some rest, good food, hot showers, and most of all to see my loved ones.

The morning finally came when it was time for my departure. I was to be processed and flown from Bien Hoa. Currently located at the squadron NDP not too far from Saigon, it was my plan to catch a ride on the resupply convoy that had arrived at our position early that morning. I found a place on what I believe was the mail jeep. Having delivered its load, the vehicle was fairly empty. It was brought to my attention that one of the convoy vehicles had struck a landmine on the way to our position. I immediately transferred boxes and bags from other vehicles and piled them in the back of the jeep. I had learned from experience that riding on a significant protective barrier would greatly lessen the chance of injury from a land mine. One would be blown well into the air, but was less likely to be injured. It was probably a strange sight seeing me perched high on the cargo as we left the NDP. No one laughed. They all understood that I was going to do everything possible to make it to my R and R. The same rules applied to soldiers ending their tours and headed home.

Upon arrival at the Bien Hoa processing center, I was given a departure time several hours away. I was issued a tooth brush and a small tube of what tasted and felt like a metal grinding compound. I was told to brush for a specified length of time. It was not pleasant but apparently was meant to remove any plaque build-up because of poor hygiene and lack of dental care in the field. I suppose it did some good, but always suspected it removed a lot of tooth enamel.

I soon found my way to the first real shower in seven months. The water pressure was good, the water was hot, and I could stay in the shower as long as I wanted. What a pleasure. It was disappointing in one way. I had a great tan from months in the sun and very limited or no protective clothing. Upon emerging from the shower, I was as pale skinned as a newborn baby. Apparently the tan was really a layer of dirt and grime I had been unable to remove with my feeble attempts to cleanse myself in the field. That setback of course, was not going to interfere with my R and R. I was on a mission.

I should have had a Khaki uniform for travel. I was told it had been destroyed in attack on our base camp where the uniform and my other personal goods were stored. I have always suspected that it was really stolen by some rear area jerks.

I was not allowed to travel in my field fatigues. Fortunately, there was a small post exchange available where I could purchase civilian clothes for travel. The outfit I acquired was not what I would normally choose. I managed to find a pair of fluorescent green slacks and an ugly shirt that fit. Shoes were a different story. The only ones available were much too small for me, but I could squeeze them onto my feet. I did not care. My parents were bringing some of my clothes from home. I would have traveled in a burlap bag if that had been the only way to get there.

It was a long flight with a stop in either Guam or Okinawa. When we reached beautiful Hawaii, I found my way to our hotel. I soon learned my parents and girlfriend had not yet arrived. Eventually I saw them emerging from a taxi. I rushed to them and gave and received big hugs all the way around. I was probably quite a sight in my ridiculous clothes, pale skin, and overwhelming joy. I'm certain that I did not appear to be the image of a dashing young officer fresh from the war zone. I did not care. I was in a safe place with at least some of my loved ones.

The time in Hawaii was absolutely fantastic. We toured the many beautiful sights on the island of Oahu and enjoyed each other's company. For the most part I was able to put the war out of my mind and enjoy the peace and comforts.

Although the food was outstanding in Honolulu and I was fortunate enough to find the joys of Guava Juice, there was one thing missing. I thought I had to have a McDonald's hamburger to really feel like home. I did and it was not very good as usual. Still, I would not have been happy if I had not fulfilled that urge for a piece of home.

One occasion resulted in extreme embarrassment to me. It was late in the evening a day or two before the New Year holiday. We were strolling peacefully through the city streets, enjoying a cool breeze, and window shopping. Someone decided it would be a good time to set off a string of firecrackers in celebration. Without thinking, I immediately hit the concrete. It is amazing how much the sound of the firecrackers echoing through the streets sounded so similar to rapid fire AK-47 rounds. You can take the boy out of the war but it takes a while to take the war out of the boy.

A high point for me came on Waikiki Beach on a moonlit evening. My girlfriend had been faithful in writing to me and was a great source of hope and comfort to me. After much thought, I asked her to marry me when I got home. I told her I would not want to marry her while we were in Hawaii. It would not be fair to family and friends. What I really meant, but did not say, was that I still had a lot of war to experience and did not want her to be a widow. She said yes and I was thrilled beyond words. Upon my arrival home the following May, she informed me things had changed. She had been offered a management internship with a large company and wanted to pursue a career rather than marry. I was hurt but have always appreciated the fact that she did not send me a "Dear John" letter while I was still deployed. She remained a source of hope and comfort throughout my tour. I know now it was for the best. I have enjoyed a wonderful wife and family for over forty two years.

Alas, the day arrived when it was time to return to S. Vietnam. I put on the crummy clothes in which I had arrived and said my goodbyes at the Honolulu Airport.

I did not really mind returning to the combat zone except for having to leave my loved ones behind. The hard part came as the airplane began its departure down the runway. I looked out the side window and was able to see my loving father. He had made his way to a high observation deck and was waving goodbye profusely. We were close enough that I could plainly see he was crying uncontrollably. I had never before seen him cry. He was a strong man and a combat veteran. He knew the dangers and hardships ahead of me. That experience strengthened my resolve to do my duty and return home to my loved ones.

The flight was uneventful and I soon found myself back at the squadron NDP performing my duties as HHT commander forward. Nothing had changed at the NDP. Five months to remain in the combat zone.

CLEAN UP

"'Tis not ours to reason why. 'Tis ours to do or die."

We had occupied the squadron NDP for several weeks. Because of the heavy foot and vehicle traffic, the area was void of vegetation. It was composed of a rough circle a few hundred yards in diameter.

We received orders to move the NDP to another area in pursuit of a new mission.

When most of the vehicles and personnel had departed for the new position, as HHT Commander Forward I was left with a few vehicles and a small contingency to clean the area.

What we saw before us was bare red earth and some minor amounts of trash.

Please note that we had been shelled numerous times in that position and that the enemy surely knew our main force had moved on.

I could hardly believe what I was hearing when I received the order to sweep the area. A helicopter even delivered a number of brooms to be used to sweep the barren ground.

You may have guessed that shortly after we began literally sweeping the area, we received a parting gift of numerous incoming rocket and mortar rounds. Fortunately, no one was hurt and we were able to complete our task of cleaning the area.

I had never heard the term politically correct, but I was glad we could keep the "tree huggers" happy. Seriously, I was glad to get out of there without sustaining casualties.

3/11 STAND DOWN

The time had finally arrived. The Eleventh Cavalry Regiment after several years of distinguished service in S. Vietnam and Cambodia received orders to leave the combat arena. After many campaigns and much hardship, the withdrawal of forces in the arena resulted in the regiment's partial deactivation.

All units were ordered to return to the regimental base camp at Dian. There we began the necessary preparations to turn in and account for all equipment and make arrangements for the lucky troopers who had enough time in country to go home and the remaining troopers to be assigned to other units.

The task of turning in thousands of combat vehicles, weapons, and other equipment seemed monumental. Of course, it was our mission to get it done.

As HHT commander forward, it was my duty, among many others, to coordinate the turn in of all Third Squadron equipment and buildings. One would think that the task would be fairly straight-forward. It was not. Over the years there had been many lapses in the record keeping resulting in significant discrepancies between what the books said we should have and what we really had. Some of the discrepancies were due to combat losses not properly recorded and others were due to theft by other units. Equally difficult to account for were the many items we had acquired over the years that were either above our allowances or had not been properly documented. We had to turn in only what we were supposed to have and nothing we were not supposed to have. What a dilemma. What would they do if we could not figure it out? Send us to Vietnam?

As in any such situations, the sergeants were invaluable. Many had friends in other units who were more than happy to accept our excess. Often trades would be arranged to ensure we had the equipment we were short. Maybe not the ideal situation, but blind eyes were turned. That is how the army works behind the scenes.

One of the largest swaps I heard of was with a unit stationed at Vung Tau. Note that I did not really know about it until the deed was done. I only authorized two well deserving sergeants to take a few days of R and R at Vung Tau. It seems we needed two more ACAV tracks and somehow had an extra M88 tank retriever. A mystery to me how we had something extra as large as an M88 tank retriever. Must have occurred years before I got there. Anyway, after the brief R and R trip, we had the required number of ACAV tracks and were not encumbered with an extra M88. Funny how that works.

There was time for final farewells to the unit and our fellow troopers at the various officer and enlisted clubs on post. We had a number of award ceremonies to award numerous troopers for their valiant efforts. Mostly we worked hard and watched as our troops slowly but surely bid farewell to the unit.

A high point for me came early one afternoon when the HHT Commander and the Squadron Commander approached me. They informed me that I had been chosen to receive a commission in the regular army if I so desired. That was, of course, pleasing to know that they had such confidence in me. It would also be a giant step in my career path if I chose to remain on active duty. They told me to consider the offer overnight and to talk with them the next day. It was a tough night. I loved the Army. On the other hand, I desperately wanted a family and knew that if I accepted their offer that I would often be deployed on one year tours and would be required to work extremely long hours when I was not deployed. That was the Army as I knew it. Little did I know that in peacetime, things were much different for family life. After careful consideration I informed my commanders that I must decline their generous offer. They were understanding and wished me well. I have often wondered if I made the right choice, but only until I think of the wonderful life I have had with my family.

Eventually I was the only one left in my squadron. My last duty was to sign over our temporary buildings to the receiving ARVN unit. As I waited for the appointed time to arrive I became very ill. I still managed to walk through the numerous buildings to ensure nothing important had been left behind. As I walked through the squadron adjutants building, I noticed a few papers on a high shelf. Examination of the papers was a true shock to me. I had a low opinion of an administrative person and he knew it. He stood accused of writing false awards for himself and one of his buddies. To me that was about as low as one could go at the time. Regardless, the papers proved to be the approved documents awarding me a second bronze star. I will never know if they were overlooked or if they were left on purpose. In any event, I turned them in at my next unit and they were entered in my military record.

Signing over the buildings proved to be a simple tasks. A few signatures and the appropriate salutes and the deed was done without fanfare. The Third Squadron no longer existed in S. Vietnam.

MOVING NORTH

After signing over the last of the Third Squadron Eleventh Cavalry buildings, it was time to start my journey to my next unit. I was feeling very ill and did not even have transportation to Bien Hoa AFB.

I started walking, as best I could because of illness, toward the Regimental Headquarters. I knew there would still be some American forces in that area and they would be a source of help. I will still at the main base camp so I felt relatively safe even without a personal weapon, which had been turned in a day or so before.

It was with great joy that I saw a troop commander I knew drive by in a jeep. He recognized me and asked if I needed help. My reply was an absolute yes. I explained my situation briefly. He told me to get in the back of his jeep. He was also destined for Bien Hoa and was kind enough to take me to the army hospital there. GIs look out for other GIs.

I was in the hospital for several days and was diagnosed with a Fever of Unknown Origin (FUO). My fever was very high and frankly I did not have any idea what was happening a good part of the time. One thing I do remember is one afternoon one of the young female army nurses checked on me and immediately yelled for another nurse. They immediately took me to a shower stall removing all my clothes as we went. They stood there fully dressed in the cold shower to support me for quite some time. I was too weak to stand on my own. It is apparent that their simple act of kindness either saved my life or at the very least prevented further damage from the high fever. I must have been really sick. I had not seen an American girl in some time and yes I was a normal young man. I was to sick to care or be embarrassed. Those young nurses will always be heroes to me.

Upon release from the hospital, I reported to the processing station. There I was given orders directing me to Fifth Mechanized Division along the DMZ. A small room was assigned to me and I was told to report to the Air Terminal every afternoon to check on availability of flights to the North.

The three day stay there until I could get a flight was not bad. There was an air conditioned movie theater and a mess hall near my quarters.

I will never forget the flight to the north. It was, of course, a military cargo plane, which I found to be very noisy and quite frankly scary. Adding to the problem was the presence of a 105 mm howitzer tied down with chains and a large number of ARVN and Vietnamese families being transported for reasons known only to those of higher grade than I held. After the plane was finally loaded, the pilot taxied down the runway and took off. We could not have been far off the ground when the plane jolted violently and I am sure came dangerously close to stalling. The howitzer had suddenly shifted about a foot on its chains. The pilot soon got the plane under control. In a few minutes, the pilot left the cockpit and counseled the ranking crewman in the rear of the aircraft. It was much too noisy to hear what was said, but from the demeanor of the two individuals it did not include language suitable for family entertainment. I bet that crewman never again failed to properly secure cargo.

It was a long and generally uncomfortable flight culminating at *Quang Tri*. *Quang Tri* was the Fifth Mechanized Infantry Division Headquarters.

I spent the evening in a large room with a number of other officers awaiting assignment. The following day I received orders to proceed a few miles up the road to Dong Hoa. My new assignment was to the Fifth Mechanized Infantry Armored Cavalry Squadron.

S-3 AIR

I was quickly processed and interviewed by a captain in the rear headquarters. He told me I would be the new S-3 Air. S-3 Air is responsible for planning and reporting on air operations. I informed him that I knew nothing about the S-3 Air duties and he informed me that I would soon learn. End of conversation.

Without delay I was put on a helicopter to the forward fire base where the squadron commander and executive officer were located. It was on a hill somewhere in the Khe Sanh Valley and was seeing more than enough action with the enemy.

I dismounted and ran in search of the squadron executive officer. He was a very tired looking man and obviously quite busy. As a staff officer, I knew I would theoretically report directly to him. I finally got his attention and without hesitation he demanded to know who I was and what the "blank" I wanted. I answered that I had been assigned as his new S-3 Air. He exploded, to put it mildly. He informed me that he was the one who made such assignments and he knew nothing about me. He was interrupted, we were in combat, and he told me to find a place on one of the perimeter ACAVs and he would sort things out in the morning. I had been told to return on the helicopter that brought me, but he outranked the captain and the helicopter had already departed anyway.

I found a track with room for me and spent the night pulling my share of guard duty, firing an M79 grenade launcher when necessary, and getting what information I could about the area and the unit from the troopers on the track.

The next morning I reported to the command track to find the executive officer in a much better mood. I was introduced the commander and was informed that I would be the squadron's S-3 Air.

I soon caught a helicopter flight back to the squadron base camp and got settled in. It was not a bad place. There was a mess hall and I shared a small room with another lieutenant.

Duty as the S-3 Air was not difficult, but like all things in a combat zone, came with risks. At the end of the first day, after spending most of the day getting settled in, came my first challenge. The squadron commander had returned to the base camp for the purpose of attending the daily staff briefing. Without warning I was told to present a briefing on current air operations. I had absolutely no knowledge of what the activities had been that day or what was planned for the next day. Fortunately, the air operations NCO came to my aid and was able to present the current status. After the briefing, the squadron commander firmly but kindly told me what was expected of me. It was never a problem thereafter.

About a month after entering my new assignment, I was summoned to the Fifth Division Headquarters. The commanding general liked to interview all his officers and it was my turn. He reviewed my file and we talked briefly about my combat experience. He seemed satisfied and asked if I needed anything personally. I told him I was doing well, but had not received pay or mail in about six weeks. It sometimes takes a while for the army systems to catch up when you are reassigned. He instantly became furious and yelled for his Adjutant General, I believe, to come in his office. The general did not use very nice language and ordered the poor fellow to take care of my pay and mail discrepancies. I received partial pay that afternoon and had a large delivery of my mail within a day or so. When the general barks, people tend to get things done.

On a typical day I would be briefed on planned air operations by the air operations NCO and would either approve or question the plan. I really had little input since the operations required were dictated by missions and availability of helicopters. I would then normally catch a ride on one of the resupply Huey helicopters and carry messages or direct the delivery of resupply to the various troop and platoon locations. It sounds simple but I had to stay aware. Messages and supplies had to get to the right place. The troopers needed them to survive and perform their various missions.

Many of the flights were peaceful. I would simply sit on top of the mound of supplies in the helicopter and enjoy the ride. From the moment we would leave base camp, we had a view into North Vietnam, on a few occasions we could see their flag flying over an outpost. A strange war, we were not allowed to cross the border or shoot over the border. The scenery was beautiful and the air was cool. We often received enemy fire, but thanks to the skill of the helicopter pilots and just plain luck, we were never hit.

The flights were always up the Khe Sanh Valley. It was a long valley with a small river and high forested hills on both sides. My first surprise was the "Rock Pile." It was a large rock formation at the base of the valley and was a notorious hiding place for VC machine guns. Several times we received fire from the "Rock Pile." The green tracers were unmistakable. The pilots would fly at various altitudes and routes for safety, but their corridor was very limited. I was amazed on one occasion when the pilot chose to fly just a few feet above the river. The VC obviously had preplanned fires and almost brought us down with mortar fire relying on the rocks and shrapnel to hit us as we flew so low. They were cunning and knew a lot of tricks to get us.

The flights over the Khe Sanh Valley reminded me of scenes from World War II. The fight for Khe Sahn at the head of the valley was furious and ongoing. The sole road to the area ran generally along the valleys edge and was always filled with resupply convoys of troops headed for Khe Sahn. Smoke, tracers, and the dust from explosions could usually be seen at many points along the way. Ambushes were common as the VC attempted to disrupt our supply efforts. I had seen a lot of combat, but this was my first overall view from the sky above.

Most of our drop-offs of supplies to the various units were fairly routine although our gunners and pilots were always vigilant. On one occasion as we approached the drop off point, it became apparent that the receiving platoon was under heavy attack. Normally we would simply return after the firefight. No need to unnecessarily risk a perfectly good helicopter and crew. The platoon leader radioed the pilot that he had wounded troopers. There was no hesitation, the pilot immediately descended to the platoon position. I furiously threw the units resupply provisions out of the helicopter while we hovered two or three feet above the ground. The helicopter crewmen were busy firing their machine guns into the forest around the platoon's position. Simultaneously, troopers on the ground carried two wounded soldiers and threw them into the helicopter. My heart would have stopped in fear but there wasn't time. I saw the "green basketball" pass under the door opening and I am sure above the helicopter skids. I knew from past experience that the "green basketball" was an incoming rocket propelled grenade (RPG). Too close for comfort. We lifted off and flew directly to the field hospital at *Quang Tri*. One of the helicopter crewman was a medic, or at least had some training. He took the lead in caring for the wounded troopers as best he could. At one point he asked me to use my fingers to put pressure on a wound in a trooper's upper leg. He guided my fingers into the wound and I held them there until we arrived at the field hospital. I have always wondered and hoped that the young trooper made it.

My tour of duty as S-3 Air vastly broadened my knowledge of military staff functions and I have always felt that I contributed at least somewhat to accomplishment of the mission. The time was not always pleasant, but was well spent.

KHE SAHN

What an incredibly beautiful sight. The valley was lush green and a mist hung over the falls. Not the kind of scenery one was accustomed to seeing in the war zone. Yet those were my thoughts the first time I rode in a helicopter over Khe Sahn Falls.

The falls were at the upper end of the Khe Sanh Valley and only a short distance from the American fire base located on a large hill. The fire base was established to protect the valley and more importantly to provide a point of interdiction on the Ho Chi Minh trail. The Ho Chi Minh trail was perhaps the most important North Vietnamese supply route for the battles to the south.

The first view of the Khe Sanh Firebase was in stark contrast to that of the falls. The position of the fire base had long been contested. As a result of thousands of rounds of incoming artillery fire and numerous battles, the firebase appeared to be a large area of greyish mud and trash. It was completely void of vegetation.

Fortunately, I did not make many trips to the fire base at Khe Sahn. One trip, however, is deeply etched in my memory. We received a mission late in the evening on a day that had been rainy and cool. As the helicopter was taking off from base camp I could not help but notice a large "Panic Button" mounted on the dashboard. Of course, this was a novelty item but turned out to be an omen. Shortly into the flight a flashing red light indicated a problem with transmission oil pressure. I knew enough to be aware that this was not a good thing. If the transmission failed, the helicopter would be without power and uncontrollable at best. The pilots discussed the problem and came to the conclusion that they could probably continue to fly. They were kind enough to explain the situation to me over the intercom system. They explained that they knew the mission was important and that they thought we could make it safely.

As we flew up the valley, several thunderstorms caused us to fly around them using precious time and fuel. Upon arrival we found a heavy thunderstorm over Khe Sanh, which prevented us from landing. More precious fuel was burned and dark was fast approaching. The thunderstorm finally cleared and we thought we were safe to land. Wrong assumption. The fire base was sustaining a heavy artillery attack. The pilots conferred and advised me that we were landing anyway. They did not feel they had enough fuel to return to base camp and more thunderstorms had developed along the route back to our base camp. I was just a passenger, but I knew we were in a tough situation.

The pilots landed the aircraft and we all immediately ran to the nearest bunker. What poor luck. We were met by a soldier aiming his M-16 rifle at us. We were denied access. It turned out to be the command bunker and no unauthorized personnel were allowed. He gruffly told us to try a bunker about fifty yards across the barren ground. Incoming shells and adrenalin enabled us to run very fast. The bunker was empty so we settled in for the night. It was a dirty place but provided us with badly needed protection. A hot cup of coffee would have certainly been a nice amenity.

After the shelling stopped, or at least slowed, I carefully approached the command bunker again. I handed the guard the package I carried that was the prime reason for the mission. I will never know if it contained cupcakes from home or battle orders. It did not matter. The mission was accomplished.

The next morning was sunny and bright. We departed the area and flew to a refueling station somewhere on the road down the Khe Sanh Valley. It was not an encouraging site. Two skeletons of destroyed helicopters laid alongside of the refueling pad. We were told the transmission froze on one and flung enough debris to destroy the other. We soon refueled and were on our way back to base camp. It was certainly good to be home.

I was proud of the pilots of the helicopter. As usual, the pilots did whatever was necessary to support the troops on the ground.

THE INFANTRY MAJOR

One evening, when I was serving as S-3 Air near the DMZ (demilitarized zone) between South Vietnam and North Vietnam, I headed for the mess hall to get some supper.

After getting my tray of food, I entered the seating area and saw an Infantry Major I had previously known as a Captain. He had been an instructor at one point in my training and I deemed him to be a friendly and outgoing professional. I will not share his name in order to preserve his privacy.

I approached him and introduced myself as it had been a long time since we had met and I was one of his many students. He nodded and uttered something like "I know who you are."

It struck me odd that he did not invite me to join him since he was seated alone. Somehow, I sensed that I should not ask to join him. He had obviously recently come from the field. His clothing was dirty and he appeared to be in a state of total exhaustion. Instead of his smile, to which I was accustomed, his face was expressionless and his eyes were sunken with no glimmer of light to them.

As I started to walk away, he stopped me. Very briefly he explained that he was an infantry battalion commander and had just returned from a long and difficult operation. He did not go into detail, but he made it clear, that he had experienced many casualties for which he appeared to blame himself. Instead of the strong leader I knew him to be, I believe he was at least temporarily a broken man. When he had finished his brief statement he looked down at his food as if it were a signal for me to go.

As I walked away, I was fairly certain that I saw tears in the strong man's eyes.

I sincerely hope that he was able to go past his immediate sorrow and depression to once again be an effective officer and to lead a happy life. Some were able to do so and some were not.

Please do not in anyway think that I saw him in a lesser light. Strong combat leaders are sometimes simply faced with burdens that even the strongest cannot always withstand. It is my observation that such men are able to function through the crisis and then collapse or fall apart emotionally when the job has been done. Most are able to rise again and probably be even stronger as a result of their experiences.

HOMEWARD BOUND

The day finally arrived. My "short-timers" calendar only had one day remaining. It was my turn to go home.

Good byes were said to my friends, paperwork was completed, and my personal weapon was turned in to the armorer. I hitched a ride on a jeep to *Quang Tri* where I found a place in the back of an uncovered two and one-half ton truck to complete my journey to Da Nang AFB. The ride was uncomfortable and I worried that, just as my initial transport when I had arrived in country, most of us were unarmed. I'm sure we were safe, but after a year with my weapon in combat, I was very uncomfortable without it at my side. As we rode, I could not help but wonder what the stories were of the others beside me.

Upon my arrival at Da Nang I processed and was told to go to a large barracks to await notification that I had been assigned a seat on a flight home. I found a bunk and was soon pleasantly surprised to see two friends who had been platoon leaders with me at Fort Hood, Texas. They too were ready to go home. We spent about two boring days and nights before receiving our seat assignments. We knew we were in a reasonably safe environment and enjoyed the lack of responsibility and the opportunity to catch up on some long lost sleep. We had access to a mess hall and spent most of the days in an officer's club that actually had air conditioning and flush toilets. We talked about our experiences and our dreams of what home would be like for us. One of the friends was very disappointed in his tour of duty. He had been assigned convoy duty in a very safe area and had heard only one gun shot in the distance. The other friend and I said nothing, we both knew what experiences he had missed.

At last we got our flight assignments and were ready to board the aircraft. We were forced to undergo a "pat down" inspection and were given the opportunity to place anything that might be considered contraband in a large barrel. I placed a large knife in the barrel that I had brought with me from home. I knew it was perfectly legal, but I wanted no chance of missing the flight if there was any question. The whole process was demeaning, but we were soldiers, and had to go along with it.

We finally boarded the commercial aircraft and gave a resounding cheer when the aircraft lifted off of the runway. We were out of Vietnam. Almost everyone on board did experience one disappointment. We had not seen pretty American girls in so long and were looking forward to seeing the pretty young stewardesses. Little did we know that stewardesses were assigned flights based on their seniority. The youngest was probably in her late forties, which of course, was ancient to us. They treated us a little too well. I knew I wasn't quite home yet when a stewardess insisted on placing a pillow behind my head followed by patting me on the head and saying "There Honey." I was a combat soldier and not ready to be treated like a small child. I know she meant well. As we crossed the international date line, I realized that I was officially promoted to the rank of Captain. I did not pin the rank on until later, but it felt good to know my promotion date had arrived.

After stops in Guam and Hawaii, the plane finally arrived in the state of Washington, I caught a taxi late in the evening to Sea-Tac Airport just outside of Seattle to begin the final leg of my journey home. Upon arrival I picked up my ticket and was told to be at the gate at six o'clock the following morning. My friend and I would be taking separate flights from there. We were dirty from the long travel and both needed to shave and brush our teeth. I had somehow managed to find a set of Khakis to wear on the trip and they were wrinkled, but nothing I could do. I came to love the USO then and there. The USO lady gave us each a bar of soap, a toothbrush and toothpaste, and a disposable razor. It wasn't all we needed but it sure did make us feel better.

Finally it was time to go to the gate for my departure. Upon arrival, I found that I had been given the wrong time and that the plane had departed. I was furious, but finally found someone to help me get the next flight. It seemed that most of the people did not really care that I had been gone a year fighting for them. I later found that observation to be generally correct. As it turned out, the flight was a connecting flight in Wichita, Kansas that connected to the same plane I would have been aboard had I caught the first flight. I arrived in Oklahoma City on schedule. I was seated toward the back of the plane beside a very nice business man. He, of course, asked me why I was traveling. After explaining my circumstance, he looked at me and simply said "thank you." That meant a lot to me. As the plane came to a stop at the gate, everyone, of course, packed the aisle and retrieved their carry-on luggage. I was anxious but knew I had to wait just a little bit longer. To my surprise, the business man yelled out in a very loud voice something similar to the following: "This man has been away for a year fighting for you. Please step aside and let him see his family." To my amazement, the aisle cleared almost instantly. I think some were showing their appreciation and others were simply intimidated. I didn't care, Home was just on the other side of that aircraft door.

HOME AT LAST

The Aircraft door was opened. As I descended the ramp, I was thrilled to see my mother and father, my brother and his family, and my fiancé. As I neared them, my brother sent my two nephews running forward to greet me. They were very young and would know me only by the picture my brother kept in their living room. The picture showed me in Army Green and now I was in a Khaki uniform. You guessed it, they ran right past me. No problem, hugs, tears and laughter abounded. I really was home.

My parents drove me to their house and we spent a wonderful afternoon visiting and laughing. The surroundings were strange to me. I had not been that comfortable and relaxed in a long time. I clearly remember going to the kitchen and opening the refrigerator. I just stood there staring at the contents. My mother came into the kitchen and asked what I was doing. I was somewhat embarrassed and told her the truth. I was in awe at the small things so readily available. It was clear I would have some adjusting to accomplish.

At one point, my father took me to the garage. There sat my shiny new Pontiac Lemans. Dad had sent me all the literature, and on my instructions, purchased my dream car so it would be waiting for me when I got home. I was able to pay for it with money I had placed in savings during my overseas tour.

I had about a month of leave before reporting to Fort Polk, Louisiana for my next assignment. It was a great time visiting family and friends. The only bad time was when my fiancé informed me that she no longer wanted to marry me. I will always think well of her for waiting until I got home to tell me rather than just sending a "Dear John" letter. She had been a great source of support and hope during my deployment. Of course, it turned out for the best. I later met my precious Linda who has been my loving wife for forty-two years.

Coming home had been all that I had hoped for and then some. It seems a shame that we have to see other parts of the world and endure hardships to truly appreciate the wonderful country with which we are blessed.

EPILOGUE

It is my fervent hope that in writing my story, I have been able to convey at least a small measure of the respect for those who have given so much in defense of our nation and way of life. I know in my heart that the sacrifices made in the past and those required of our current and future military services are absolutely worth the high costs that must be paid. I have had the opportunity to witness first-hand the plight of those who do not enjoy the freedoms so rarely and preciously found in the United States of America. Yes, the price is high and must be born by a relatively select few. Thankfully, we must know that the price has been paid and will continue to be paid. The phrase "Freedom isn't free" is absolutely true.

It is apparent to those who know me well that I, like all people, cannot be perfect in every way. I simply strive to always do the best I can and hope to seek to understand others. As are all people, I am the sum of my experiences and interactions with others. I perceive myself as being somewhat softhearted and fun-loving but, to a great extent, tempered with the ability to be firm and unbending when necessary. Perhaps these stories, which reveal a small but very significant portion of my life, will help others to seek to understand me and realize why I live my life as I do.

This small sampling of one man's war is intended to give insight, though seldom answers, to our current and future leaders who do or will serve in the military. Hopefully, they will recognize the importance of the actions required of them and can, in some small way, learn a few of the lessons contained in the experiences related herein. Mostly I hope they recognize the need to be prepared and the absolute fact that they can and must learn to depend on their fellow soldiers.

As to my fellow veterans, I fully understand that each of you has experienced military service different from mine. I ask only that you pause to reflect and then readily share with younger generations. One never knows when one little thing you teach them can make a huge difference. We may be too old and tired for active service, but let us use our knowledge and experience to ensure the generations to follow understand the importance and have the ability to continue the fight for the precious freedoms we have.

In the course of reliving and writing of my experiences, I freely admit to having become very emotional. So much was given by my friends and family. As a result of self-examination, I have what I believe is a better understanding of myself and why I am the way I am. Hopefully, I have been able to grow as a person.

Yes, of the millions of veterans of our armed services, each has experienced his own war. Each and every one has made a significant contribution simply by doing what was asked of him or her. Let us never forget and always strive to make things better and safer for this great land and our future generations. God bless America.

ABOUT THE AUTHOR

Early in his life, Lieutenant Colonel Charles E. "Chuck "Ferguson knew he was destined to be an Army officer. As a young boy, he voraciously read any books he could find pertaining to military figures and battles. His father, who obtained the rank of Colonel, was an inspiration and role model who set the standards high.

He was commissioned as a Second Lieutenant in 1969 and served three years active duty as an armored cavalry unit leader and various staff positions including a tour in South Vietnam and Cambodia.

Upon leaving active duty, he enjoyed about twenty-five years as a reserve officer evaluating National Guard and US Army Reserve units. During this period, he performed as a staff officer on assignments including, Fort Mead, Fort Lewis, and numerous assignments at the Pentagon.

His civilian career was varied and included retail, contracting officer for the US Air Force, and real estate development. He is currently an active real estate agent.

He has enjoyed active leadership roles in the Boy Scouts of America, numerous school support groups, Lions Club, Kiwanis, and other civic organizations.

In all his activities, he has enjoyed training and mentoring younger generations.

He currently resides in his hometown of Harrah, Oklahoma, with his wife, Linda, and enjoys his three children and their families, including four grandchildren, and is blessed with many friends.

CPSIA information can be obtained
at www.ICGtesting.com
Printed in the USA
LVOW12s1337041217
558575LV00002B/165/P